God's Vaccine

by David Eells

UBM BOOKS

© 2018 David Eells. All rights reserved. Permission is granted to copy and quote portions of this book, provided the context is accompanied with the copyright notice and contact details.

ISBN: 978-1-942008-23-1
Second Edition – Large Print Edition – 2019

Download this book and others freely from www.ubmbooks.com.

Scriptures are taken from the *American Standard Version (ASV)* because of its faithfulness to the ancient manuscripts and Bible Numerics, a system designed by God for proving authenticity.

We have departed from the *ASV* only in the name Jehovah and Lord Jehovah which we replaced with Lord and Lord God, respectively. Neither represents the original YHWH but Lord is less confusing to many and we did not want this to distract from the teaching.

Numerics is a system designed into the Bible by God to prove authenticity. The Greeks and Hebrews used their letters for numbers. Therefore, the whole Bible is also written in numbers which show perfect patterns as long as the God-inspired original words are not departed from. It mathematically proves the original text and where it has been added to or taken away from. The Numeric English New Testament (NENT) is based on the numeric pattern and is quoted from when necessary.

We desire to make this book free on our part because Jesus said, "Freely you have received, freely give," The E-book is freely available on our website **www.ubm1.org**. Free copies of our books are at times made available at **www.ubm1.org/free** through the generous donations of His faithful servants. When other book houses sell our materials we do not take a percentage of profits when their rules make this possible as it is now. Other houses that we may use in the future demand the author/UBM receive at least the lowest percentage. When this happens that money will go towards free books in agreement with the Lord's command as we have done in the past.

ACKNOWLEDGEMENTS

May our Father bless those whom He used to create this book from transcriptions of David Eells' teachings:
- Jessica McGinley who created the cover art.
- Many brothers and sisters who have worked on this book but do not wish any credit.

Books of the Bible - Abbreviation List

Old Testament

Gen.	Genesis
Exo.	Exodus
Lev.	Leviticus
Num.	Numbers
Deu.	Deuteronomy
Jos.	Joshua
Jdg.	Judges
Rth.	Ruth
1Sa.	1 Samuel
2Sa.	2 Samuel
1Ki.	1 Kings
2Ki.	2 Kings
1Ch.	1 Chronicles
2Ch.	2 Chronicles
Ezr.	Ezra
Neh.	Nehemiah
Est.	Esther
Job.	Job
Psa.	Psalms
Pro.	Proverbs
Ecc.	Ecclesiastes
Son.	The Song of Solomon
Isa.	Isaiah
Jer.	Jeremiah
Lam.	Lamentations
Eze.	Ezekiel
Dan.	Daniel
Hos.	Hosea
Joe.	Joel
Amo.	Amos
Oba.	Obadiah
Jon.	Jonah
Mic.	Micah
Nah.	Nahum
Hab.	Habakkuk
Zep.	Zephaniah
Hag.	Haggai
Zec.	Zechariah
Mal.	Malachi

New Testament

Mat.	Matthew
Mar.	Mark
Luk.	Luke
Joh.	John
Act.	Acts
Rom.	Romans
1Co.	1 Corinthians
2Co.	2 Corinthians
Gal.	Galatians
Eph.	Ephesians
Php.	Philippians
Col.	Colossians
1Th.	1 Thessalonians
2Th.	2 Thessalonians
1Ti.	1 Timothy
2Ti.	2 Timothy
Tit.	Titus
Phm.	Philemon
Heb.	Hebrews
Jas.	James
1Pe.	1 Peter
2Pe.	2 Peter
1Jn.	1 John
2Jn.	2 John
3Jn.	3 John
Jud.	Jude
Rev.	Revelation

TABLE OF CONTENTS

    Preface 6

1. Separating From Egypt..7
2. Disqualifications for Christ's Passover 35
3. Abiding in the Secret Place of the Most High.........63
4. Believe the Truth and Be Set Free! 91
5. How to War Against Fear...116
6. God's Wondrous Protection and Provision 143
7. Anxiety and Fear, Part 1 168
8. Anxiety and Fear, Part 2 198
9. Steps You Can Take to be Immune from Plagues and Pestilences 221

PREFACE

Please note that this book is compiled from audio broadcasts given over the course of approximately two years. There is, therefore, some duplication between the chapters in order to maintain the integrity of the individual teachings.

Where a word or concept may be new to the reader, an explanation is generally provided with the first occurrence thereof. Unless otherwise indicated, all Scripture quotations are taken from the American Standard Version.

Punctuation also has been simplified so as not to distract the reader. For example, when Scripture is quoted, brackets have been omitted where they would commonly be used to indicate that a lower case letter has been capitalized, the ellipsis has been shortened to three periods where it would commonly be a set of four to indicate that a partial text is being cited, and so forth.

I pray the Father will use this book to both edify and encourage every reader.

The Editor

CHAPTER ONE

Separating From Egypt

Dear Father, we thank You for being our Savior in all things. We thank You, Lord, that we can turn to You and put our faith in You in these tumultuous times. You have provided everything through Jesus Christ. He has totally borne our curse according to Galatians 3:13. You've taken the curse of sin and of death and have put it upon Him, Lord. You have blessed us because of our Passover Lamb. You have set us free and have provided us everything necessary to protect us in this world. Lord, we thank You. We thank You, Lord, for what You're doing to raise up Your children as sons of God in these days to demonstrate the provision of Your great salvation. Lord, the world needs to see a people who believe Your Word and stand upon Your Word. The world needs to see a people who have the blessings of protection and provision and healing and deliverance that You provided at the Cross, Lord. We thank You for it, Father, in Jesus' Name. Hallelujah!

Repentance Brings Separation

The government and pharmaceutical companies are making a big push to get everybody to take immunization shots for just about everything they can think of, from the flu and allergies to shingles and all the vaccinations they give babies these days. But God has another plan for His people because there's a difference between them and the world. God has His Own "immunization," His Own "vaccination." When the time came for God to free His people and lead them out of Egypt, which in type represents the world, He had to use some of the curses that He poured out in Egypt on His people, too (Exodus 3:7). He had to do that to bring His people to repentance so He could separate them. They went through the curse of the waters being turned to blood (Exodus 7:20), the plague of the frogs (Exodus 8:6), and the plague of the lice (Exodus 8:17), but by the time of the plague of the flies (Exodus 8:24), the Lord finally seemed to have gotten His people's attention enough to where He could actually separate them from Egypt. ***(Exo.8:22) And I will set apart in that day the land of Goshen, in which my people dwell, that no swarms of flies shall be there; to the end thou mayest know that I am the Lord in the midst of the earth. (23) And I will put a <u>division between my people and thy people</u>: by tomorrow shall this sign be. (24) And the Lord did so: and there came grievous swarms of flies into the house of Pharaoh, and into his servant's houses: and in all the land of Egypt the land was corrupted by reason of the swarms of flies.*** Praise God! We need that separation again today. It hasn't happened to the overall church yet, but it's been happening on an individual basis. As people repent of self-willed rebellion, as they repent of trusting in the world and the arm of the flesh, they're being separated. As they turn to God by faith in what He said in His promises, they're being separated. I'm convinced that's what separates us from Egypt and puts us in Goshen. That separation is so important that He emphasizes it by repeating it a little further on. ***(Exo.11:7) But against any of the children of Israel shall not a dog move his tongue, against man or beast: that ye may know how that <u>the Lord doth</u>***

make a distinction between the Egyptians and Israel.

After the Red Sea crossing and the miraculous provision of the water being made sweet at Marah (Exodus 15:22-25), the Lord told the Israelites, *(Exo.15:26) ... If thou wilt diligently hearken to the voice of the Lord thy God, and wilt do that which is right in His eyes, and wilt give ear to his commandments, and keep all his statutes, I will put none of the diseases upon thee, which I have put upon the Egyptians: for I am the Lord that healeth thee.* Well, He is not only "the Lord that healeth thee," but He is "the Lord that 'vaccinates' you"; He is "the Lord that 'inoculates' you." Contrary to popular opinion, the Lord is in control of all plagues, all diseases, and so on. He has ultimate authority. He may use vessels of dishonor, such as the devil and spirits of infirmity, to chasten people and to bring them to repentance so that they can have God's blessings, but it's still the Lord and it's still His purpose that is fulfilled. He *(Eph.1:11) ... worketh all things after the counsel of his will* and *(Dan.4:35) ... none can stay his hand, or say unto him, What doest thou?* John the Baptist said, *(Joh.3:27) ... A man can receive nothing, except it have been given him from heaven.* So we need to believe what the Lord says here, "I will put none of the diseases upon thee, which I have put upon the Egyptians; for I am the Lord that healeth thee."

The World's "Cures" Bring a Curse

Many people are panicking, trying something here and trying something else over there, wondering what they can do to defend themselves against a curse that God ordained. I tell you that there's nobody who can get rid of a curse that God ordains except God Himself, but there are certainly many people who try. Even a lot of the vaccinations and inoculations that man gives just move the curse from one place to another. You haven't actually gotten rid of the curse, you've just traded it for something else. At any rate, once we realize God is in control, then we understand that we need to be separated from "Egypt," because the Lord has His own "vaccination" against the curses, His own Passover from the plagues of this world. The Lord told the Israelites for each household to take a lamb and slaughter that lamb (Exodus 12:3), and we know that that "lamb" is Jesus Christ. He is our Passover Lamb. ***(1Co.5:7) Purge out the old leaven, that you may be a new lump, even as ye are unleavened. For our passover also hath been sacrificed, [even] Christ: (8) wherefore let us keep the feast, not with old leaven, neither with the leaven of malice and wickedness, but with the <u>unleavened bread</u> of sincerity and truth.*** Truth sets you free. Truth is Jesus Christ. ***(Joh.8:31) Jesus therefore said to those Jews that had <u>believed him</u>, If ye abide in my word, [then] are ye truly my disciples; (32) and ye shall know the truth, and <u>the truth shall make you free</u>.*** Jesus Christ has already been sacrificed in order that we may have a Passover. We don't have to literally go and slaughter a lamb for this. We can accept and believe in the Lamb Who was sacrificed, Jesus Christ.

The Unleavened Bread and the Passover Lamb

As a type and shadow, we're told about the Passover in the Old Testament. *(Exo.12:5) Your <u>lamb</u> shall be without blemish, a male a year old* (We know that was Jesus.)*; ye shall take it from the sheep, or from the goats; (6) and ye shall keep it until the fourteenth day of the same month; and the whole assembly of the congregation of Israel shall kill it at even. (7) And they shall take of the blood, and put it on the two side-posts and on the lintel, upon the houses wherein they shall eat it. (8) And they shall eat the flesh in that night, roast with fire, and <u>unleavened bread</u>; with bitter herbs they shall eat it.* So "unleavened bread" represents the same thing that the "lamb" does, because Jesus Christ is the Word of God. *(Joh.1:1) In the beginning was the Word, and the Word was with God, and the Word was God.* And, *(Joh.6:51) I am the living bread which came down out of heaven: if any man eat of this bread, he shall live for ever: yea and the bread which I will give is my flesh, for the life of the world.* The "unleavened bread" is the Word of God without adding what men usually add to it or taking away what men usually take away from it. Many people love to add their ideas in there to make it more palatable for the flesh to be able to receive it. Unleavened bread doesn't taste like much, but with just a little leaven, it tastes a whole lot better to the flesh.

Obviously, the Lord is saying to us, "No, no, I want you to eat unleavened bread." In fact, He instituted seven days of unleavened bread from this point on until the Israelites had actually left Egypt. In type, those last seven days represent the seven years of the tribulation period, which are to be days of unleavened bread before leaving this world, as represented by Egypt. God is going to demand in the last seven days that His people do not touch "leaven" and there's a harsh penalty if they do. ***(Exo.12:15) Seven days shall ye eat unleavened bread; even the first day ye shall put away leaven out of your houses: for whosoever eateth leavened bread from the first day until the seventh day, <u>that soul shall be cut off from Israel</u>.*** That is a dire threat from God. He's saying, "Okay, you have one more chance. This is the end. We don't want anybody sitting on the fence because the lukewarm are going to be spewed out. Don't accept any leaven. Accept nothing but the true Word of God. Depart from your evil ways and your false religion and your ideas of prosperity. Depart from everything that you're adding to my Word in order to let the flesh live." You see, when we eat unleavened bread, it's supposed to be a crucifixion to the flesh. The unleavened bread is Jesus Christ, the Lamb, the Word, and He warns us not to add to it the leaven of the Pharisees, which is religion, or the leaven of Herod, which is government (Mark 8:15). Neither one should we trust in. We already have a Savior, and He is Jesus Christ. We're also told to eat the lamb with bitter herbs (Exodus 12:8). ***(Rev.10:9) And I went unto the angel, saying unto him that he should give me the little book. And he saith unto me, Take it, and eat it up; and <u>it shall make thy belly bitter</u>, but in thy mouth it shall be sweet as honey.*** So it's bitter to the flesh, and it's supposed to be bitter to the flesh.

(Exo.12:9) Eat not of it raw, nor boiled at all with water, but roast with fire; its <u>head</u> (This is

Separating From Egypt

talking about the Mind of Christ.) **with its <u>legs</u>** (This is talking about the walk of Christ.) **and with the <u>inwards</u> thereof** (And this is talking about the Heart of Christ). We are to eat everything that is Christ, all of the Lamb. We reject nothing in the Word because it's all been given for a Passover and this is how we <u>keep</u> the Passover. If you're somebody who's caught up in religion, just going around in religious circles, you need to go get your Bible and read it. Make sure you know what it says, especially all of the New Testament. If you're only getting one or two verses in a sermonette on Sunday, you're not getting enough to protect you from what's coming, especially the plagues that are coming down the road. You need to get all of the Word down in your heart. **(Exo.12:10) And ye shall let nothing of it remain until the morning; but that which remaineth of it until the morning ye shall burn with fire.** (We will lose what we don't eat, and so we won't have a full Passover. A word not acted on is a word forgotten and lost.) **(11) And thus shall ye eat it: with your loins girded, your shoes on your feet, and your staff in your hand...** In other words, be ready to leave Egypt and to separate yourself from the Egyptians when you eat this Word. Don't try to drag this Word back into the world with you, instead, come out of the world and follow God. Be ready to move.

The Old Man and the New Man

(Exo.12:11) And thus shall ye eat it: with your loins girded, your shoes on your feet, and your staff in your hand; ye shall eat it in haste: it is the Lord's passover. (12) For I will go through the

land of Egypt in that night, and will smite all the first-born in the land of Egypt... The "first-born" is the flesh. ***(1Co.15:46) Howbeit that is not first which is spiritual, but that which is natural; then that which is spiritual.*** First comes the natural and then the spiritual; the fleshly man is born first and then the spiritual man is born again. God is going to take out the "old man" in us and He's going to take out the world because they are also the "old man," and if we live after the "old man" of the world, He's going to take us out. We have to repent of religion. We have to change our mind by eating the unleavened bread. When you eat something, it goes into you and becomes who you are. Remember that Jesus said, ***(Joh.6:51) I am the living bread which came down out of heaven: if any man eat of this bread, he shall live for ever: yea and the bread which I will give is my flesh, for the life of the world.*** He is the "Manna" in the wilderness. He is the Unleavened Bread. We partake of Him because there is nothing else that can give us life and nothing else that can give us a passover, but Jesus and His Word. Give up on religion, folks. They all had to do it in Jesus' day. They all had to come out and they all had to follow Him. They were the *ekklesia*, "the called-out ones." They came out of all their religions and they followed Jesus.

It is the Lord We Must Fear, Not Satan

(Exo.12:12) For I will go through the land of Egypt in that night, and will smite all the first-born in the land of Egypt, both man and beast; and against all the gods of Egypt I will execute

judgments: I am the Lord. In other words, everything that men today trust in, God will judge. It will all be found false. It will all be found a failure. It will all be found to be nothing you can put your trust in. ***(13) And the blood shall be to you for a token upon the houses where ye are; and when I see the blood, <u>I will pass over you</u>*** (Notice He said, "I will pass over you." We think about the death angel passing over, but the Lord said, "I will pass over you."), ***and there shall no plague be upon you to destroy you, when I smite the land of Egypt.*** We've already had a few "smitings," folks, but we're getting very close to seeing some major judgments coming down the road and God is saying, "If you will just do this, no plague will be upon you. If you will just repent and hold fast to the Word and let the Lord be your Passover, then no plague will be upon you to smite you when I smite the land of Egypt." It is the <u>Lord God</u> doing this. Fear Him only; don't fear man or the devil. So we see that He will give us seven "days" of this unleavened bread before leaving "Egypt," and that anyone eating leavened bread during that time would be cut off.

(Exo.12:23) ***<u>For the Lord will pass through to smite the Egyptians</u>; and when he seeth the blood upon the lintel, and on the two side-posts, <u>the Lord will pass over the door</u>, and will not suffer the destroyer to come in unto your houses to smite you.*** It's the <u>Lord</u> Who is passing over and it's the <u>Lord</u> Who doesn't permit the destroyer to smite you. The Lord has complete control over the destroyer at all times. If there is a plague, it is because the Lord is permitting the destroyer to judge the Egyptians, but He does not want the destroyer to judge you. He would rather that you repent and eat the lamb, the unleavened bread. He would rather that you be inoculated by God and have your protection from God, your Exodus 15:26 protection from God. That's awesome! All through the Scriptures, we see more of this promised protection (Psalm 91; Mark 16:18; Luke 10:19; Acts 28:5; etc.), and we see who <u>can</u> have it and who <u>cannot</u> have it.

Deny the Flesh

So the Lord says that all we need is the unleavened bread, but the old man of the flesh just wants more flesh and the flesh can't protect anybody from the curse. Well, the Israelites in the wilderness murmured against the Lord's plan for them. ***(Num.11:6) But now our soul is dried away; there is nothing at all save this manna to look upon.*** They had gotten sick of manna. It was certainly keeping them alive and keeping them healthy, but their flesh lusted for something more than the manna. God was saying, "No, this is all you need," and they were complaining, "We want something more. We want what we had back in Egypt." ***(Num.11:4) And the mixed multitude that was among them lusted exceedingly: and the children of Israel also wept again, and said, <u>Who shall give us flesh to eat</u>? (5) We remember the fish, which we did eat in Egypt for nought; the cucumbers, and the melons, and the leeks and the onions and the garlic; (6) but now our soul is dried away; there is nothing at all save this manna to look upon. (7) And the manna was like coriander seed, and the appearance thereof as the appearance of bdellium. (8) The people went about, and gathered it, and ground it in mills, or beat it*** *in mortars, and boiled it in pots, and made cakes of it: and the taste of it was as the taste of fresh oil.* They probably cooked the manna in every kind of way you can imagine that you could make manna. The transliteration of the Hebrew word *manna,* by the way, is "man," and Jesus said, *(Joh.6:33) For the bread of God is that which <u>cometh down out of heaven</u>, and giveth life unto the world. (35) ... <u>I am the bread of life</u>: he that cometh to me shall not hunger, and he that believeth on me shall never thirst. (38) For <u>I am come down from heaven</u>, not to do mine own will, but the will of him that sent me.* Jesus is the Word made flesh (John 1:14).

(Num.11:10) And Moses heard the people weeping throughout their families, every man at the door of his tent: and the anger of the Lord was kindled greatly; and Moses was displeased. Moses didn't know what to do and he cried out to the Lord. *(13) Whence should I have flesh to give unto all this people? For they weep unto me, saying, Give us flesh, that we may eat. (14) I am not able to bear all this people alone, because it is too heavy for me.* Then the Lord told Moses, *(18) And say thou unto the people, Sanctify yourselves against tomorrow, and ye shall eat flesh; for ye have wept in the ears of the Lord saying, Who shall give us flesh to eat? For it was well with us in Egypt: therefore the Lord will give you flesh and you shall eat. (19) Ye shall not eat one day, nor two days, nor five days, neither ten days, nor twenty days, (20) but a whole month, until it come out at your nostrils, and it be loathsome unto you; because that*

***ye have rejected the Lord who is among you*, and have wept before him, saying, Why came we forth out of Egypt?"** He said they "rejected the Lord" because when they rejected the manna, they rejected Jesus Christ, the "bread of heaven" (Exodus 16:4; Psalm 105:40; John 6:51; etc.). They rejected the "bread" that had no leaven of the Pharisees and no leaven of Herod (Mark 8:15). They didn't want the unleavened bread, instead they wanted to partake of flesh and, if you remember, that's why Esau sold his birthright. **(Heb.12:16) ... Or profane person, as Esau, who for one mess of meat** (That's obviously the flesh in type; he sold out to the flesh.) **sold his own birthright.** Well, that's a type here, too. The Israelites were doing the same thing.

(Num.11:31) And there went forth a wind from the Lord, and brought quails from the sea, and let them fall by the camp, about a day's journey on this side, and a day's journey on the other side, round about the camp, and about two cubits above the face of the earth. That's a lot of quail! And to blow them in from the sea by a wind across the wilderness to bring them there is just amazing. Nothing can stop God from providing for us, but we don't want to depart from the type that He's giving us here, which is the flesh. The Israelites wanted flesh, so He told them, "Therefore the Lord will give you flesh and you shall eat ... until it come out at your nostrils, and it be loathsome unto you." **(Num.11:32) And the people rose up all that day, and all the night, and all the next day, and gathered the quails: he that gathered least gathered ten homers: and they spread them all abroad for themselves round about the camp. (33) While the flesh was yet be-**

tween their teeth, ere it was chewed, the anger of the Lord was kindled against the people, and the Lord smote the people with a very great plague. Now we see who was <u>not</u> protected from the plague: it was those who partook of a fleshly word. The manna represented the true Word, but they wanted their word to be leavened by the flesh so it would let the old man live. They wanted a word that pleased their flesh. Of course, God is not angry with people eating quail. The parable here is that it's death to depart from the pure Word of God. Anything added by man, whether through dead religion or whether by patriotism toward any government, is adding things of man to make the unleavened bread more acceptable to the flesh. We are not to trust in any of these things. Everybody in every religion, when Jesus came the first time, had to come out from among them (2 Corinthians 6:17) to follow Him. *(Joh.10:2) But he that entereth in by the door is the shepherd of the sheep. (3) To him the porter openeth; <u>and the sheep hear his voice</u>: and he calleth his own sheep by name, and leadeth them out. (4) When he hath put forth all his own, he goeth before them, <u>and the sheep follow him</u>: for they know his voice. (5) And a stranger will they not follow, but will flee from him: for they know not the voice of strangers.* They had to depart from the leaven, totally depart from the leaven, to walk after the Lamb.

In this case, God was angry because they were lusting after flesh. They wanted a word that would please their flesh and the text goes on to prove that. *(Num.11:33) While the flesh was yet between their teeth, ere it was chewed, the anger of the Lord was kindled against the people, and the Lord smote the people with a*

very great plague. (34) And the name of that place was called <u>Kibroth-hattaavah</u>... The Hebrew there means "the graves of lust," and what is going to happen to those people who lust after the flesh? The plague will be upon them. They will not be able to escape it, but the Lord said that if you eat His Lamb, if you eat His unleavened bread, there will be a passover. He will not permit the destroyer to come into your home to destroy you. He says the opposite here; He says that those who lust after the flesh will not escape the wrath of God. ***(Num.11:34) And the name of that place was called Kibroth-hattaavah, because there they buried the people that lusted. (35) From Kibroth-hattaavah the people journeyed unto Hazeroth: and they abode at Hazeroth.*** So there's the parable and that's what the Lord wanted us to see. He is a mighty God, a mighty Savior, but He wants us to eat what's good for us.

What can you <u>do</u> about the plagues that are coming? You need to eat the Lamb so there will be a passover of the destroyer for you, and to "eat the Lamb" is to accept only what God says. ***(Rom.4:5) But to him that worketh not, but <u>believeth on him that justifieth the ungodly</u>, his faith is reckoned for righteousness.*** God will accept you as being righteous if you will just repent of believing anything but <u>His</u> Word. Through numerics, God put hidden patterns in the Bible so that we can prove the Bible is actually His Word, but we can't prove anything that <u>men</u> say the Lord has spoken. Nothing. Their opinions are worthless to God and their opinions are worthless to bring forth Christ in us. Only His Bread can bring forth ***(Col.1:27) ... Christ in you, the hope of glory***, because He is the Word. He's not man's word, He's God's Word. So we accept only God's Word, and since faith is accounted as righteousness until righteousness is manifested, God will accept you. When you've repented and turned away from men and their doctrines and you've turned to Him in your faith, God accounts you as righteous. Praise God! If you're accounted as righteous, then you have a Blood covering. The Bible says, **(1Jn.1:7) ... *if we walk in the light*** (The "light" is the unleavened bread; it's partaking of the Lamb.)**, *as he is in the light, we have fellowship one with another, and the blood of Jesus his Son cleanseth us from all sin*** (Of course, "sin" is "unrighteousness."). Wow! And if you have a Blood covering, then there's no curse on you. **(Psa.91:10) *There shall no evil befall thee, Neither shall any plague come nigh thy tent.***

Judgment for Rebellion

A little later on, even though God through Moses had already judged the Israelites once, there was a rebellion in the camp by Korah, Dathan, and Abirum. So God sent an earthquake to prove that Moses was the true leadership and that these people were usurpers, apostates who didn't have the true Unleavened Bread. **(Num.16:31) *And it came to pass, as he made an end of speaking all these words, that the ground clave asunder that was under them; (32) and the earth opened its mouth, and swallowed them up, and their households, and all the men that appertained unto Korah, and all their goods. (33) So they, and all that appertained to them, went down alive into Sheol: and the earth closed upon them, and they perished from among the assembly. (34) And all Is-***

rael that were round about them fled at the cry of them; for they said, Lest the earth swallow us up. (35) And fire came forth from the Lord, and devoured the two hundred and fifty men that offered the incense. Then these self-deceived people blamed Moses for the earthquake, as if <u>Moses</u> could crack the earth open and swallow them up. They had completely lost all common sense. *(Num.16:41) But on the morrow all the congregation of the children of Israel murmured against Moses and against Aaron, saying, Ye have killed the people of the Lord. (42) And it came to pass, when the congregation was assembled against Moses and against Aaron, that they looked toward the tent of meeting: and behold, the cloud covered it, and the glory of the Lord appeared. (43) And Moses and Aaron came to the front of the tent of meeting. (44) And the Lord spake unto Moses, saying (45) Get you up from among this congregation, that I may consume them in a moment...* God had had enough. When plagues come and wipe out a lot of God's people, as happened in quite a few places in the Scriptures (Genesis 7:21-23,19:24-25; 1 Chronicles 21:14; Lamentations 4:6; etc.), it was because God had had enough. Does He ever get that way today? <u>Yes</u>, He does. He's very merciful, He's very long-suffering, as the Bible says, but there comes a time when people have counted on His long-suffering and have found it was not there anymore. You see, God has to do something when people are in willful rebellion and yet they think they're going to heaven. God has to come and make a clear separation between what's flesh and what's manna. He has to make that separation, and He usually has to punctuate it with a judgment of some kind.

(Num.16:45) Get you up from among this congregation, that I may consume them in a moment. And they fell upon their faces. (46) And Moses said unto Aaron, Take thy censer, and put fire therein from off the altar, and lay <u>incense</u> thereon, and carry it quickly unto the congregation, and make atonement for them: for there is wrath gone out from the Lord; the plague is begun. Well, I submit to you at this particular time in history, that the "plague" has begun and it is coming forth now. It's time for God's people to separate from the apostasy and the leaven of the Pharisees and get themselves in a position where God will defend them. I believe that the "incense" here, as most people believe, is intercessory prayer. *(Jas.5:16) ... The supplication of a righteous man availeth much in its working.*

(Num.16:47) And <u>Aaron</u> took as Moses spake, and ran into the midst of the assembly; and behold, the plague was begun among the people: and he put on the incense, and made atonement for the people. (48) And he stood between the dead and the living; and the plague was stayed. The root verb of the Hebrew name "Aaron" means "to be light or to give light; shine," and we learned earlier that "walking in the light" is the same as "walking under the Blood of the Lamb," the Covering (1 John 1:7). We also learned that you have the Covering only if you're partaking of the Lamb, only if you're exercising faith in what He accomplished for you at the Cross. He took away your sins and He took away your curse at the Cross. If you believe that, and are not walking in willful disobedience, then you have the Blood covering.

The Covering is for Those Who Believe the Full Gospel

Most of the church doesn't have that Covering. They would be wiped out in a plague because they don't believe that the Lamb <u>bore</u> the curse. **(Gal.3:13)** <u>**Christ redeemed us from the curse of the law, having become a curse for us**</u>**; for it is written, Cursed is every one that hangeth on a tree: (14) that upon the Gentiles might come the blessing of Abraham in Christ Jesus; that we might receive the promise of the Spirit through faith.** That's one way to be preserved through a plague; you believe the full Gospel, not a half Gospel as most churches out there do. You believe the full Gospel that Jesus Christ, Who is our High Priest (Hebrews 2:17,3:1,5:10,etc.), not only delivered you from the sin, but He delivered you from the curse of the sin. If you don't believe that, you are not entitled to escape plagues. By the way, the Hebrew word *nega* translated "plague" just means "an affliction, a stroke." It doesn't necessarily always mean a "disease." So here we see that their high priest Aaron, whose name means "light," ran out between the living and the dead. That was a dangerous thing to do but he knew he was safe. God's true people, who walk in the light, know that. They know they're safe from any plague but the rest don't know that. The rest don't have that cleansed conscience because of the promises of the Word (1 John 3:21). They're too busy playing church to have time to get in the Word for themselves and find out what it really says. Well, that can be a deadly mistake. **(Num.16:49) Now they that died by the plague were fourteen thousand and seven hundred, besides them that died about the matter of Korah. (50) And Aaron returned**

unto Moses unto the door of the tent of meeting: <u>and the plague was stayed</u>. The plague stopped right there. Aaron took that incense and put it in his censer and he went out there and it stayed the plague. He made atonement, or "at-one-ment," if we just break down the spelling. He made the people "one with God." Aaron could do that because of what he represented; he represented the Light. He represented a man who walked in Light. He was "enlightened" and "lighted."

Confess Your Sins

(Jas.5:14) Is any among you sick? Let him call for the elders of the church; and let them pray over him, anointing him with oil in the name of the Lord: (15) and the prayer of faith shall save him that is sick, and the Lord shall raise him up; and if he have committed sins, it shall be forgiven him. (16) Confess therefore your sins one to another, and pray one for another, that ye may be healed. The supplication of a righteous man availeth much in its working. We can see the same two things there, repentance and faith. Confess your sins. This is a very good thing to do. Many people just want to have faith, but I say confess your sins and then believe. It also says, "The supplication of a righteous man availeth much in its working," and that's what we just saw with Aaron. I submit to you that these people didn't deserve deliverance from this plague, and the fact was, it was wiping them out, but a righteous man stood in the midst and he offered his incense, his prayer, and God stopped right there. He wasn't going to go over that righteous man because he wasn't under the plague. He wasn't going to go through that righteous man because he wasn't under the plague. Aaron stood in the gap, he made up the hedge (Ezekiel 22:30), and God honored his act of faith and the plague was stayed at only 14,700, besides those who were wiped out in the Korah, Dathan, and Abirum rebellion.

Standing in the Gap

(Jas.5:17) Elijah was a man <u>of like passions</u> (That means "of like nature.") **with us, and he prayed fervently that it might not rain; and it rained not on the earth for three years and six months. (18) And he prayed again; and the heaven gave rain, and the earth brought forth her fruit.** Notice that, yes, we can have faith for ourselves, we can be diligently walking after the Lord, but also, God can use us to defend people who are not worthy of deliverance from some plague. He can use us to be an atonement for people who would normally be wiped out. He can use our prayers to save them, so we need to be somebody whom God would respect. I would say of most people who would have gone out there in the midst of the plague, God would have rolled right over them and taken them out because they were not worthy. They were not "light" as Aaron was Light. **(1Jn.1:7) ... If we walk in the <u>light</u>, as he is in the <u>light</u>, we have fellowship one with another, and <u>the blood of Jesus his Son cleanseth us from all sin</u>.** The Blood covering was certainly upon Aaron. God defended him and the people behind him. He stood in the gap, and they were saved. They were very unworthy and God had already decided to wipe them out, and so it is with a lot of the church today. There is much rebellion against God. What is God going to do? In some cases, He'll use you to defend people who are quite unworthy.

(1Ki.8:37) If there be in the land famine, if there be pestilence, if there be blasting or mildew, locust or caterpillar; if their enemy besiege them in the land of their cities; <u>whatsoever plague</u>, whatsoever sickness there be, (38) what prayer and supplication soever be made by any man, [or] by all thy people Israel, who shall know <u>every man the plague of his own heart</u>, and spread forth his hands toward this house... In a way, this is applying "plague" to the "plague of a person's own heart." The Bible says, ***(3Jn.1:2) Beloved, I pray that in all things thou mayest <u>prosper</u> and be in health, even <u>as thy soul prospereth</u>.*** Many times, the plague comes because of what's in a person's heart. ***(1Ki.8:39) Then hear thou in heaven from thy dwelling-place, and forgive, and do, and render unto every man according to all his ways, whose heart thou knowest; for thou, even thou only, knowest the hearts of all the children of men (40) that they may fear thee all the days that they live in the land which thou gavest unto our fathers.*** Praise the Lord! The Lord is saying He will accept prayer for His people. He will accept the righteous prayer of a righteous man, and He will defend and He will deliver because of that, and not necessarily that the people deserve it. If you are the only one in your family that knows the Lord, God can use you to defend your family the same way Aaron was defending his family here. It's very important that we, who know the Lord, walk under the Blood, forsake the leaven of the world, and serve the Lord in righteousness so that God will respect our prayers when these times of judgment come around our loved ones.

(Lev.26:13) I am the Lord your God, who brought you forth out of the land of Egypt, that <u>ye should not be their bondmen</u> (We've been set free from bondage, the old man. Romans 6 says twice that He made us free from sin and He delivered us out of the power of darkness.)***; and I have broken the bars of your yoke, and made you go upright.*** The people whom God would judge more than any other are the people who have <u>been</u> set free, but decide of their own free will to serve the flesh, to feed on the flesh. These are the people ***(Luk.12:48) ... to whomsoever much is given, of him shall much be required...*** The world doesn't have any freedom. You can expect them to sin because that's their nature; that's what sinners do. Christians, the people who have been given freedom but instead choose to sin, these are the ones to whom God sends judgment.

The Sin of God's People Brings Plague

(Lev.26:14) But if ye will not hearken unto me, and will not do all these commandments; (15) and if ye shall reject my statutes, and if your soul abhor mine ordinances, so that ye will not do all my commandments, but break my covenant; (16) I also will do this unto you: <u>I will appoint terror over you</u> (And God is surely doing that in these days.) ***even consumption and fever, that shall consume the eyes, and make the soul to pine away; and ye shall sow your seed in vain, for your enemies shall eat it. (21) And if ye walk contrary unto me, and will not hearken unto me, I will bring seven***

times more plagues upon you according to your sins. The main reason plagues come is because of the sins of God's people. *(22) And I will send the beast of the field among you, which shall rob you of your children, and destroy your cattle, and make you few in number; and your ways shall become desolate. (23) And if by these things ye will not be reformed unto me, but will walk contrary to me; (24) then will I also walk contrary unto you; and I will smite you, even I* (The Lord wants you to understand that He's the One doing this. It's not the conspiracies of men, not even bad men who made bad vaccines; it's God.), *seven times for your sins. (25) And I will bring a sword upon you, that shall execute the vengeance of the covenant...* It was the curse of the Covenant. God's Covenant is not only blessing, it's also a curse. God's Word is not only blessing, it's also a curse. God said that He will execute vengeance upon the person who "will not hearken unto me."

(Lev.26:25) And I will bring a sword upon you, that shall execute the vengeance of the covenant; and ye shall be gathered together within your cities: and I will send the pestilence among you... Of course, the most common place for pestilences to come is in cities because that's where a lot of people are gathered together. It's easy for infections to spread in close quarters. Most of the judgments spoken about in the Bible will come upon cities, as we can see even from this passage right here. *(25) And I will bring a sword upon you, that shall execute the vengeance of the covenant; and ye shall be gathered together within your cities: and I will send the pestilence among you; and ye shall be delivered into the hand of the enemy. (31) And I will*

***make your cities a waste**, and will bring your sanctuaries unto desolation, and I will not smell the savor of your sweet odors. (32) And I will bring the land into desolation; and your enemies that dwell therein shall be astonished at it. (33) And you will I scatter among the nations, and I will draw out the sword after you: and your land shall be a desolation, and **your cities shall be a waste**.*

*(Deu.28:15) But it shall come to pass, if thou wilt not hearken unto the voice of the LORD thy God, to observe to do all his commandments and his statutes which I command thee this day, that all these curses shall come upon thee, and overtake thee. (16) Cursed shalt thou be in the city and cursed shalt thou be in the field. (17) Cursed shall be thy basket and thy kneading-trough. (18) Cursed shall be the **fruit of thy body*** (This is speaking of your children.) *and the fruit of thy ground.* Many times the curse will fall upon the children of believers who are walking in rebellion. There it is; it's very plain. People will ask, "Why has this happened to my son?" Or, "Why is my daughter having to go through this?" Well, that wasn't a judgment on their child, it was a judgment on them. And a child may even be taken away but it will be a judgment upon the parents, because when a curse comes upon the child, it comes upon the parents. We have to walk with the Lord for our "fruit" to be blessed.

It is the Lord that Sends the Plagues

(Deu.28:21) The Lord will make the pestilence cleave unto thee, until he have consumed thee

from off the land, whither thou goest in to possess it. When we read the chapter, we see it goes on to speak one curse after another but I'm going to skip on down because there's a point I'd like to make about these curses. *(58) If thou wilt not observe to do all the words of this law that are written in this book, that thou mayest fear this glorious and fearful name, THE LORD THY GOD; (59) then the Lord will make thy plagues wonderful, and the plagues of thy seed, even great plagues, and of long continuance, and sore sicknesses, and of long continuance. (60) And he will bring upon thee again all <u>the diseases of Egypt</u>, which thou wast afraid of; they shall cleave unto thee.* All the diseases that are going around today, from the flu to the Zika virus to diabetes to cancer and on and on, these are "the diseases of Egypt" that are <u>not</u> supposed to be coming upon the people of God. "The diseases of Egypt" are only able to come upon God's people when they do not hearken unto His Word and they do not fear His Name. *(61) Also every sickness, and every plague, which is not written in the book of this law, them will the Lord bring upon thee, until thou be destroyed.* It takes <u>pages</u> to tell you how many judgments will come upon the people.

(Eze.14:19) Or if <u>I send a pestilence</u> in to that land... Again, notice it's always the Lord Who is doing this. People like to say, "It's the devil. The devil is doing this and the devil is doing that." No, it's the Lord. It's His authority and only His authority. He's the only sovereign One and *(Joh.3:27) ... A man can receive nothing, except it have been given him from heaven.* That's what the Bible says. If you're going to <u>believe</u> the Bible, you're go-

ing to believe the unleavened bread. If all you see is the devil behind everything, then you fear the devil. Jesus told us not to fear the devil or any man. He said to fear Him. *(Mat.10:28) And be not afraid of them that kill the body, but are not able to kill the soul: but rather fear him who is able to destroy both soul and body in hell.* And, *(Jas.4:7) Be subject therefore unto God; but resist the devil, and he will flee from you.* Of course, if we understand that ultimately everything we have to deal with in our life comes from Him, then we will fear Him and we will know what we have to do. We have to please Him; we don't have to please anybody else.

(Eze.14:19) Or if I send a pestilence into that land, and pour out my wrath upon it in blood, to cut off from it man and beast; (20) though Noah, Daniel, and Job, were in it, as I live, saith the Lord, they should deliver neither son nor daughter; they should but deliver their own souls by their righteousness. There's going to come a time when God won't even accept your prayers for other people, no matter how righteous you are. *(21) For thus saith the Lord: How much more when I send my four sore judgments upon Jerusalem, the sword, and the famine, and the evil beasts, and the pestilence, to cut off from it man and beast! (22) Yet, behold, <u>therein shall be left a remnant</u> that shall be carried forth...* So the Lord may wipe out a lot of people, and He may wipe out a lot of His people because that's what He's talking about here, but there will be a remnant of God's people that will not be touched by these plagues. *(22) Yet, behold, <u>therein shall be left a remnant</u> that shall be carried forth, both sons and daughters: behold, they*

shall come forth unto you... Why has this remnant escaped the plague? Remember we just got through reading that "they should but deliver their own souls by their righteousness." There's a lot of deception going on. The problem with the people of God today is that they don't know who is righteous and who isn't. There's a lot of confusion out there as to who's right and who's wrong. Everybody thinks that their particular religion is right and all the others are wrong, but only those who eat the unleavened bread, only those who walk in the Light, have the truth.

After the plague passes through, God has a lesson for us. ***(Eze.14:22) Yet, behold, <u>therein shall be left a remnant</u> that shall be carried forth, both sons and daughters: behold, they shall come forth unto you, and <u>ye shall see their way and their doings</u>...*** What does that mean, "You're going to see their way and their doings"? It means you're going to see what righteousness really looks like, because those who escape the plague are truly the righteous people. ***(22) And ye shall be comforted concerning the evil that I have brought upon Jerusalem, even concerning all that I have brought upon it. (23) And they shall comfort you, when you see their way and their doings*** (We want to see those people who are righteous and pure and holy before God, because that's what we need to be.)***; and ye shall know that I have not done without cause all that I have done in it, saith the Lord.*** Yes, when you see the difference between those who are righteous and those who are not, when you see the difference between the remnant who are left and those who were wiped out, then you know that God did what was right, He did what was just, and, of course, He always does.

Submitting to the Word is God's Vaccine

Folks, wouldn't you like to know what that difference is <u>before</u> the judgment comes, <u>before</u> the plague passes through? We've been warned that it's about to pass through but God has given us His vaccination, His inoculation. It is to <u>submit</u> to His Word. It is to <u>eat</u> His unleavened bread. It is to <u>live</u> under the Blood covering, to be <u>walking</u> in righteousness and truth. When people see that the plagues pay no attention to what church somebody belongs to, when people see that the unrighteous have no answer and no defense against the plagues as they pass through, it will make an impression on them. When people see that those who believe the Bible, and refuse to depart from the Word of God even though they're called "criminals" and "heretics," when they see that these people escape, it will make an impression on them. I guarantee you, then they will know those who God thinks are righteous, but we've already seen here what that is. We've seen God sent the plague upon those who lusted after the flesh, who permitted doctrines that appeased their flesh and tickled their ears, that told them only what they wanted to hear. We need to make sure that we don't depart from the Word to run after the flesh. We have to read the Bible like we've never read it before, and we have to repent by ***(2Co.10:5) casting down imaginations, and every high thing that is exalted against the knowledge of God, and <u>bringing every thought into captivity to the obedience of Christ</u>***. We need to throw out anything we've been taught, anything we believe, that doesn't agree with the Word.

CHAPTER TWO

Disqualifications for Christ's Passover

 Father, in the Name of Jesus, we thank You, Lord, for being our God and for drawing us into Your midst. We thank You for causing us to abide in Jesus Christ, our Savior. Lord, show us what it means to eat the Passover Lamb. Show us what it means to have Your Word living in us, to be the Word made flesh, as our Lord is the Word. Show us the privileges that come from this manifestation, Lord. We ask it in the Name of Jesus. This is most important to us, Lord, and we thank You for it, we thank You, as always, for everything. Amen.

God's Vaccine Has No Bad Side-Effects

 We're learning about God's "vaccination," and we discovered that one of the ways God explains it in the Bible is here. ***(Exo.12:13) And the blood shall be to you for a token upon the houses where ye are: and <u>when I see the blood</u>, I will pass over you, and <u>there shall no plague be upon you to destroy you</u>, <u>when I smite the land of Egypt</u>.*** We found out that the qualification to have this vaccination of the Lord where no plague would destroy us, is that we have to eat all of the Lamb. Our cells are made out of what we eat, and all that is a parable for us to understand that we are to assimilate the Word of God so that it becomes who we are. Obviously, this is a vaccination with no bad side-effects!

 There is no curse upon the Word of God. There is no curse upon the Lord, Jesus Christ, and He's called the "Word of

God" (John 1:1). "Christ in you," is, of course, the "hope of glory" (Colossians 1:27). We slaughtered the Lamb some 2,000 years ago. ***(1Co.5:7) ... For our passover also hath been sacrificed, [even] Christ.*** He was sacrificed to bear the curse, the penalty, for us. ***(Gal.3:13) Christ redeemed us from the curse of the law, having become a curse for us...*** so that we could partake of the benefits of His Word, and escape from the curses of this world. For instance, the plagues were upon Egypt (Exodus chapters 7-11), but when they sacrificed the lamb of God and partook of that sacrifice, they had a Passover of the destroyer. The Lord said that when He smote the land of Egypt, His people would escape (Exodus 12:13). No plague will be near our house; no plague will be on us to destroy us. Praise God! That's our vaccination and the person who eats all of the Lamb is qualified to receive it. Of course, that means we don't want to reject any of God's Word. We want to believe all of God's Word so we can be completely protected by the vaccination. Sadly, there's a major part of Christianity that doesn't believe Jesus paid the penalty for their curse so that we would escape (Galatians 3:13). They're not really partaking of the Passover, because that's the particular part of the sacrifice that we really need to believe. ***(Rom.4:5) But to him that worketh not, but believeth on him that justifieth the ungodly, his <u>faith is reckoned for righteousness</u>.*** Faith is accounted as righteousness and if you are righteous, then you are not under the curse. In the previous chapter we looked at what it takes for somebody to qualify for this vaccination from the Lord, and now I'd like to look at what would disqualify them from getting it.

The Idol of "Another Jesus"

There's a very interesting story in Jeremiah which tells us about this, and it's a prophecy of the times we're entering into right now. **(Ecc.1:9) That which hath been is that which shall be; and that which hath been done is that which shall be done: and there is no new thing under the sun.** All we have to do is look back through history and we will be able to see what God is going to do, because history repeats. We just saw what God is going to do about vaccinating His people, and we just saw that those who do not eat the Lamb will be disqualified from receiving His vaccination because they're not assimilating the Word of God into their life. They may be justifying themselves. They may be making up a "God" that's not the real God of the Bible. They may be making up doctrines that permit them to live in the flesh. All of those things will create an idol, but that idol isn't going to save them. **(Isa.45:20) ... they have no knowledge that carry the wood of their graven image, <u>and pray unto a god that cannot save</u>.** The Bible warns us, **(2Co.11:4) For if he that cometh preacheth another Jesus, whom we did not preach, or if ye receive a different spirit, which ye did not receive, or a different gospel, which ye did not accept, ye do well to bear with [him].** And it doesn't matter if it's "another Jesus" or "another gospel." **(Gal.1:6) I marvel that ye are so quickly removing from him that called you in the grace of Christ unto a different gospel; (7) which is not another [gospel] only there are some that trouble you, and would pervert the gospel of Christ. (8) But though we, or an angel from** *heaven, should preach unto you any gospel other than that which we preached unto you, let him be anathema. (9) As we have said before, so say I now again, if any man preacheth unto you any gospel other than that which ye received, let him be anathema.* Neither "another Jesus" or "another gospel" is able to save, and when the time comes, that will be found out because the wind and the waves are coming to prove the house, whether it's on the sand or upon the rock (Matthew 7:24-27; Luke 6:46-49). Praise be to God!

    Let's begin where the Lord complains, first of all, that His people have followed after other gods. *(Jer.19:13) And the houses of Jerusalem, and the houses of the kings of Judah, which are defiled, shall be as the place of Topheth, even all the houses upon whose roofs they have burned incense unto all the host of heaven, and have poured out drink-offerings unto other gods.* God's people had become idolaters and He said that these places would be as the place of Topheth. Well, Topheth was the place where they burned the trash and where they buried criminals. It's very symbolic of those who don't obey God and are idolaters. *(Jer.19:14) Then came Jeremiah from Topheth, whither the Lord had sent him to prophesy; and he stood in the court of the Lord's house, and said to all the people, (15) Thus saith the Lord of hosts, the God of Israel, Behold, I will bring upon this city and upon all its towns all the evil that I have pronounced against it; because they have made their neck stiff, that they may not hear my words.* They are not assimilating the Word of God, not eating the Lamb, and because of that, they're not qualified to escape the judgments of God.

Disqualifications for Christ's Passover

He's obviously speaking, here, to that apostate city of God that He called a "harlot." *(Isa.1:21)* ***How is the faithful city become a harlot! she that was full of justice! righteousness lodged in her, but now murderers.*** He's also speaking of the leaders of that harlot.

(Jer.20:1) Now <u>Pashur</u>, the son of <u>Immer</u> the priest, who was chief officer in the house of the Lord, heard Jeremiah prophesying these things. The name "Pashur" means "released, liberation, freedom." He's the son, or the "fruit," of "Immer," which means "speaking, prominent." So Pashur is "free and prominent" and he represents here the leadership of the apostate people of God. You can imagine how little Jeremiah was liked by these people. There is no prophet of God, no holy minister of God, who has ever been liked by any apostate leaders throughout history. It was like that in Jesus' day. All the denominations of Judaism and their leaders were against Jesus, and every other man-child ministry throughout the Bible was hated the exact same way. God said that these were people who had "made their neck stiff, that they may not hear my words." ***(Jer.20:2) Then Pashur <u>smote Jeremiah</u> the prophet, <u>and put him in the stocks</u> that were in the upper gate of Benjamin, which was in the house of the Lord.*** That sounds like Joseph being cast into prison (Genesis 39:20). In our text here, you're going to see they did that to Jeremiah twice. But, you know, when Joseph came out of prison, he came out of prison to be the man-child (Genesis 41:39) that God was going to use to save God's people (Genesis 50:20), and we're going to see that be repeated here in type.

The Pattern of God's People Going into Bondage

(Jer.20:3) And it came to pass on the morrow, that Pashur brought forth Jeremiah out of the stocks. Then said Jeremiah unto him, <u>the Lord hath not called thy name Pashur</u> (His name means "free," but Jeremiah is about to tell him that "You're not going to be free.") ***<u>but Magor-missabib</u>***. The Lord gave Pashur a new name that means "terror on every side." He's saying, "You're not free because you're going to have terror on every side." ***(4) For thus saith the Lord, Behold, I will make thee a terror to thyself, and to all thy friends; and they shall fall by the sword of their enemies, and thine eyes shall behold it; and I will give all Judah into the hand of the king of Babylon...*** This is the time shortly before Babylon took God's people into captivity, so Pashur wasn't going to be free. He was going into bondage. Many times in history, we see God's people have gone into bondage just before the man-child was birthed, Jesus Himself being the chief Man-child. In Jesus' time, of course, God's people were in bondage. In Joseph's time, God's people were in bondage. In Daniel's time, God's people were in bondage. In our time, Christians think that they're going to be free, but that's not true. They will be going into bondage, not necessarily in jail, but going into bondage to the beast. They're going to lose their freedoms. We can look around us right now and we can certainly see who Babylon is, too. We can see who is the great eagle of Babylon at the head of all nations. We can see the image of the beast (Daniel chapters 2 and 3).

(Jer.20:4) For thus saith the Lord, Behold, I will make thee a terror to thyself, and to all thy

friends; and they shall fall by the sword of their enemies, and thine eyes shall behold it; and I will give all Judah into the hand of the king of Babylon, and he shall carry them captive to Babylon, and shall slay them with the sword. They're going into captivity and Pashur had a bad name, "free," because he wasn't going to be free. *(5) Moreover I will give all the riches of this city, and all the gains thereof, and all the precious things thereof, yea, all the treasures of the kings of Judah will I give into the hand of their enemies; and they shall make them a prey, and take them, and carry them to Babylon. (6) And thou, Pashur, and all that dwell in thy house shall go into captivity; and thou shalt come to Babylon, and there thou shalt die, and there shalt thou be buried, thou, and all thy friends, to whom thou has prophesied falsely.* Here is the false leadership of the apostate people of God, along with his whole house, going into captivity, going into bondage in Babylon. Jeremiah, in this text, represents the Man-child and there's been a man-child in every age.

The Man-Child is Always Hated by Unrepentant Apostates

Jesus, of course, is the Man-child, and He told us that He was coming again as a Man-child born to a woman. *(Joh.16:16) A little while, and ye behold me no more; and again a little while, and ye shall see me. (17) Some of his disciples therefore said one to another, What is this that he saith unto us, A little while, and ye behold me not; and again a little while, and ye shall see me: and, Because I go to the Father? (18) They said therefore, What is this that he saith, A little while? We know not what he saith. (19) Jesus perceived that they were desirous to ask him, and he said unto them, Do ye inquire among yourselves concerning this, that I said, A little while, and ye behold me not, and again a little while, and ye shall see me? (20) Verily, verily, I say unto you, that ye shall weep and lament, but the world shall rejoice: ye shall be sorrowful, but your sorrow shall be turned into joy. (21) A woman when she is in travail hath sorrow, because her hour is come: but when she is delivered of the child, she remembereth no more the anguish, for the joy that a man is born into the world. (22) And ye therefore now have sorrow: but I will see you again, and your heart shall rejoice, and your joy no one taketh away from you.*

So Jesus is coming in His people, and we see that again in Revelation as the beginning of the new leadership that God is going to give to His people. *(Rev.12:1) And a great sign was seen in heaven: a woman arrayed with the sun, and the moon under her feet, and upon her head a crown of twelve stars; (2) and she was with child; and she crieth out, travailing in birth, and in pain to be delivered. (3) And there was seen another sign in heaven: and behold, a great red dragon, having seven heads and ten horns, and upon his heads seven diadems. (4) And his tail draweth the third part of the stars of heaven, and did cast them to the earth: and the dragon standeth before the woman that is about to be delivered, that when she is delivered he may de-*

vour her child. (5) And she was delivered of a son, a man child, <u>who is to rule all the nations with a rod of iron</u>: and her child was caught up unto God, and unto his throne. (6) And the woman fled into the wilderness, where she hath a place prepared of God, that there they may nourish her a thousand two hundred and threescore days.

Jeremiah was called a "man-child" (Jeremiah 20:15). He bemoaned the fact that he, as a man-child, was born into this life to much sorrow, much persecution, and much trouble (Jeremiah 20:16-18). Wasn't it that way with Joseph? Wasn't it that way with Daniel? Wasn't it that way with Jesus? They all received persecution and hatred, especially from those who liked the status quo. *(Jer.20:7) O Lord, thou hast persuaded me, and I was persuaded; thou art stronger than I, and hast prevailed: <u>I am become a laughing-stock</u> all the day, <u>every one mocketh me</u>. (8) For as often as I speak, I cry out; I cry, Violence and destruction! because <u>the word of the Lord is made a reproach unto me</u>, <u>and a derision</u>, all the day.* The Word of the Lord that came out of his mouth made him infamous among apostate people, who only love to please themselves. The Word of the Lord is crucifying and the flesh fights against that; the flesh doesn't want to die. Jeremiah was obviously slandered and mocked and laughed at by those people who were in power, those people who, like Pashur, were "free" and "prominent." If you're going to follow the Lord, you're certainly not going to be famous or prominent. You'll be infamous and looked down upon, and that's what Jesus said. So, of course, Jeremiah, as the Man-child, was being hated.

(Jer.20:9) And if I say, I will not make mention

of him, nor speak any more in his name, then there is in my heart as it were a burning fire shut up in my bones, and I am weary with forbearing, and I cannot [contain]. (10) For I have heard the defaming of many, terror on every side. Denounce, and we will denounce him, [say] all my familiar friends, they that watch for my fall; peradventure he will be persuaded, and we shall prevail against him. (11) But the Lord is with me as a mighty one [and] a terrible: therefore my persecutors shall stumble, and they shall not prevail; they shall be utterly put to shame, because they have not dealt wisely, even with an everlasting dishonor which shall never be forgotten. (12) But, O Lord of hosts, that triest the righteous, that seest the heart and the mind, let me see thy vengeance on them; for unto thee have I revealed my cause. (13) Sing unto the Lord, praise ye the Lord; for he hath delivered the soul of the needy from the hand of evil-doers. Then, as we mentioned, he bemoans his life, his birth, his persecutions and the shame heaped upon him. Now look at this. *(Jer.21:1) The word which came unto Jeremiah from the Lord, when king Zedekiah sent unto him <u>Pashur the son of Malchijah</u>...* Here is another Pashur from a different father and yet, the strange thing is that both of these Pashurs, these "sons of prominence," who were free and who were leaders of God's people, persecuted Jeremiah, just as happened to Jesus in His day.

(Jer.38:1) And Shephatiah, the son of Mattan, and Gedaliah the son of Pashur, and Jucal the son of Shelemiah, and Pashur the son of Malchijah, heard the words that Jeremiah spake unto all the

people, saying, (2) Thus saith the Lord, <u>He that abideth in this city shall die</u> by the sword, by famine and by pestilence... Obviously, they haven't been inoculated. These apostate people are going to be made war upon by the king of Babylon. Jeremiah told them that if they abode with their apostate leadership in that apostate city, which was not the true city of God, that they were going to be attacked "by the sword, by famine and by pestilence." Well, I think that is a pure type and shadow for our day. These things are coming. *(Jer.38:2) Thus saith the Lord, <u>He that abideth in this city shall die</u> by the sword, by famine and by pestilence; but he that goeth forth to the Chaldeans shall live, and his life shall be unto him for a prey, and he shall live. (3) Thus saith the Lord, This city shall surely be given into the hand of the army of the king of Babylon, and he shall take it. (4) Then the princes said unto the king, <u>Let this man</u>, we pray thee, <u>be put to death</u>; forasmuch as he weakeneth the hands of the men of war that remain in this city, and the hands of all the people, in speaking such words unto them...* They wanted to stay in that city. The people who loved the status quo and their apostasy didn't want to leave, and they didn't want these words to weaken them in their war against the king of Babylon, even though God had already warned them to not war against him.

(Jer.38:4) Then the princes said unto the king, Let this man, we pray thee, be put to death; forasmuch as he weakeneth the hands of the men of war that remain in this city, and the hands of all the people, in speaking such words unto them: <u>for this man seeketh not the welfare of this people</u>,

but the hurt. Of course, Jeremiah wasn't seeking any such thing; he was seeking to be the Voice of God in order to bring them to repentance and to turn them around. In every generation, there has been that same Voice. ***(5) And Zedekiah the king said, Behold, he is in your hand; for the king is not he that can do anything against you. (6) Then took they Jeremiah and cast him into the <u>dungeon of Malchijah</u> the king's son...*** There it is a second time, the dungeon of Malchijah. Remember, he was the father of this Pashur. Once again, these princes of the people of God are throwing Jeremiah into the dungeon, into shackles. ***(6) Then took they Jeremiah and cast him into the dungeon of Malchijah the king's son, that was in the court of the guard: and they let down Jeremiah with cords. And in the dungeon there was no water, but mire; and Jeremiah sank in the mire.*** Ebed-melech, who was an Ethiopian eunuch, interceded to the king that Jeremiah would die there, and the king told him to go and pull Jeremiah up out of the well and keep him in the house (Jeremiah 38:7-13). So this is the second time we see that he was persecuted and threatened with death, and now we can continue with our text back in Jeremiah 21.

Well, the king sent this Pashur to ask Jeremiah, ***(Jer.21:2) Inquire, I pray thee, of the Lord for us; for Nebuchadrezzar king of Babylon maketh war aginst us*** (We see from Revelation 13 that the beast is going to make war on the saints.)***: peradventure the Lord will deal with us according to all his wondrous works, that he may go up from us. (3) Then said Jeremiah unto them, Thus shall ye say to Zedekiah: (4) Thus saith the Lord, the God of Israel, Be-***

hold, ***I will turn back the weapons of war that are in your hands*** (In other words, "The weapons that you think are going to defend you against the king of Babylon will fail you.") ***wherewith ye fight against the king of Babylon, and against the Chaldeans that besiege you, without the walls; and I will gather them into the midst of this city.*** He's telling them, "Your walls are not going to protect you. The king of Babylon and his warriors are coming into your city." ***(5) And I myself will fight against you with an outstretched hand and with a strong arm, even in anger, and in wrath, and in great indignation.*** I dare say that most of the people of God today would not believe, and would probably smite, any prophet who said that they were not going to be overcomers, who told them that they were going to go into bondage and that the beast was going to conquer them. Most of the people of God today would say, "No, no, I don't believe that! That's a false prophet!" Yet God is saying here, through His true prophet, that He is going to fight against them. He is going to make their weapons useless and He is going to fight on the side of the king of Babylon.

Judgment Comes to the Apostates

(Jer.21:6) And *I* will smite the inhabitants of this city, both man and beast... The Lord is doing this because of their apostasy, because of their stiff neck, because of their hatred for the Word of God. They had created a god of their own making to fall down and worship. They may have called him "Jehovah," but that didn't make any difference; it was still an idol and idols cannot save (Isaiah 45:20). As a matter of fact, God cannot answer a person who is trusting in an idol, because then He would be giving glory to the idol (Ezekiel 14:3-8) and, of course, then everybody would run to the idol. God says over and over in the Scriptures that He is not going to answer when we're in idolatry. He's not going to answer. Turn your heart to the true God of the Bible. Eat the Word of God. Assimilate what it is so that you know the true God. He is the Word. He will not change His Mind.

(Jer.21:6) And <u>I will smite</u> the inhabitants of this city, both man and beast: they shall die of <u>a great pestilence</u>. The <u>Lord</u> is bringing the pestilence against the apostates, even though here this pestilence is coming at the hand of the king of Babylon. You know, a lot of people today don't think that the pestilence is coming from the great eagle and they may find out they're wrong sooner rather than later, but however it comes, the Lord is sending it. We could waste a lot of time blaming the beast kingdom. God <u>uses</u> the beast kingdom to do what comes natural to them because that's what they were designed for by Him. It's God Who is sending the pestilence against the people of God in our very, very near future. It's coming through the king of Babylon, but it's God Who is sending it. **(Jer.21:7) And afterward, saith the Lord, <u>I will deliver Zedekiah king of Judah</u>, <u>and his servants</u>** (This is the apostate king and his servants.), **and the people, even <u>such as are left in this city from the pestilence</u>, from the <u>sword</u>, and from the <u>famine</u>, into the hand of Nebuchadrezzar king of Babylon** (The Lord is going to deliver them out of that, but only so He can deliver them into the hand of Nebuchadrezzar, who has been making war on them.)**, and <u>into the hand of their enemies</u>, and into the hand of those that seek their**

life: and he shall smite them with the edge of the sword; he shall not spare them, neither have pity, nor have mercy. There's a great crucifixion coming to the people of God because of their apostasy. Many will come to repentance and turn back to Him, possibly even as they're going to their guillotines or are on their deathbeds from pestilences. It's sad that people have to enter into the Kingdom in that way, but it's necessary so that they <u>can</u> enter into the Kingdom. Praise be to God!

When Josephus was hired by the Romans to write the history of the Jews, he said the very same situation existed then as we just read about. He said of Jesus' time and the days leading up to 70 A.D., when the Roman siege was against the Jews, that the Jews were in rebellion against God. And he believed that the reason these terrible things came upon them, this death, this destruction, this pestilence, was because of the way the Jews treated Jesus and His disciples. You might as well write in "Christian" there because there's no difference today. ***(Ecc.1:9) That which hath been is that which shall be; and that which hath been done is that which shall be done: and there is no new thing under the sun.*** The way they treat Jesus in His people is no different today. Remember He said, ***(Mat.10:40) He that receiveth you receiveth <u>me</u>, and he that receiveth me receiveth <u>him that sent me</u>.*** And, ***(Mat.25:40) ... Inasmuch as ye did it unto one of these my brethren, even these least, ye did it unto me.*** So it depends on how they treat God's representatives, as to how God is going to treat them. In Jesus' day, Josephus said it was the way the Jews treated Jesus and His disciples that caused this great judgment to fall upon them. It's no different today, folks. There are people who are going to, once again, rail against and hate God's leadership that He is sending. I'm not talking about an individual man, I'm talking about the firstfruits Man-child leadership that God is raising-up to restore the Church to the Word of God. And, once again, however they treat these people will be how they're going to be treated.

This story is found again in Jeremiah 27 and I'd like to take a look at it so that you can get the flavor of that time. This is the same king, Zedekiah, and the Lord gave Jeremiah a Word to send him through his messengers. **(4) ... Thus saith the Lord of hosts, the God of Israel, Thus shall ye say unto your masters: (5) I have made the earth, the men and the beasts that are upon the face of the earth, by my great power and by my outstretched arm; and I give it unto whom it seemeth right unto me. (6) And now have I given all these lands into the hand of <u>Nebuchadrezzar</u> the king of Babylon, <u>my servant</u>** (Nebuchadrezzar was His servant to bring under subjection, bring to their cross, the Lord's rebellious people. It was like breaking a horse to make it useful to the rider.)**; and the <u>beasts of the field</u> also have I given him to serve him.** The "beasts" were those kingdoms that were ruled over, according to Daniel chapters 2 and 3. **(7) And all the nations shall serve <u>him</u>, and <u>his son</u>, and <u>his son's son</u>, until the time of his own land come: and then many nations and great kings shall make him their bondman.** These three leaders ruled during the 70 years of the nations being conquered and the captivity of God's people under Babylon. Some people don't believe that there might be three leaders in the future for the time of the seven years of tribulation but I disagree; I think we are going to see that happen.

Disqualifications for Christ's Passover

(Jer.27:8) And it shall come to pass, that the nation and the kingdom which will not serve the same Nebuchadrezzar king of Babylon, and that will not put their neck under the yoke of the king of Babylon, that nation will I punish, saith the Lord, with the sword, and with the famine, and with the <u>pestilence</u> (There it is again; apparently the people are not qualified for the Passover vaccine.), ***until I have consumed them by his hand. (9) But as for you, hearken ye not to your prophets, nor to your diviners, nor to your dreams, nor to your soothsayers, nor to your sorcerers, that speak unto you, saying, Ye shall not serve the king of Babylon: (10) for they prophesy a lie unto you, to remove you far from your land, and that I should drive you out, and ye should perish. (11) But the nation that shall <u>bring their neck under the yoke of the king of Babylon</u>*** (This is necessary for their crucifixion.), ***and serve him, that [nation] will I let remain in their own land, saith the Lord; and they shall till it, and dwell therein. (12) And I spake to Zedekiah king of Judah according to all these words, saying, Bring your necks under the yoke of the king of Babylon, and serve him and his people, and live. (13) Why will ye die, thou and thy people, by the sword, by the famine, and by the <u>pestilence</u>, as the LORD hath spoken concerning the nation that will not serve the king of Babylon?*** That word "pestilence" keeps popping-up over and over. Obviously, those people of God who choose to war with the beast in the <u>flesh</u>, are not going to escape the judgment that's going to come through the hand of the beast. We're commanded, instead, to **(Eph.6:17) Take ... the sword of the Spirit... (Eph.6:12) For our wrestling is not against flesh and blood, but against the principalities, against the powers, against the world-rulers of this darkness, against the spiritual [hosts] of wickedness in the heavenly [places].**

Let's look at a further proof of this. **(Jer.39:8) And the Chaldeans burned the king's house, and the houses of the people, with fire, and brake down the walls of <u>Jerusalem</u>.** That is apostate Jerusalem, and when I say, "Jerusalem," I'm applying it to Christendom, too, not just the Jews. We have our own New Testament spiritual Israel and our own king David, yet, people would rather not serve Him; they would rather serve all the apostates with whom they have replaced him. **(9) Then Nebuzaradan the captain of the guard <u>carried away captive</u> into Babylon the <u>residue of the people</u> that remained in the city** (So they were taken into bondage.)**, the deserters also that fell away to him, and the residue of the people that remained. (10) But Nebuzaradan the captain of the guard left of the <u>poor of the people</u>, that had nothing, in the land of Judah, and gave them vineyards and fields at the same time.** Praise God!

Who do you think those "poor of the people" are? All the prophecies about Jesus' coming were that He would preach unto the "poor" (Psalm 35:10, 140:12; Job 5:15; Isaiah 61:1; etc.), but this is not talking about the financially poverty-stricken. **(Jas.2:5) Hearken, my beloved brethren; did not God choose them that are <u>poor as to the world</u> to be rich in faith, and heirs of the kingdom which he promised to them that love him?**

Disqualifications for Christ's Passover 53

This is talking about those who were poor as to the <u>ways</u> of the world. God choose them "to be rich in faith, and heirs of the kingdom," and notice that God provided for <u>these</u> people. But what did the Lord say about those people the world considered to be "important," such as Pashur and his whole house? The Lord said, "You're going into captivity and you shouldn't have been named 'Pashur' because you're not going to be free. You're going to have terror on every side." And this story is telling us very clearly who is going to be threatened by the terrorists in our day, because history always repeats (Ecclesiastes 1:9).

(Jer.39:11) Now Nebuchadrezzar, the king of Babylon gave charge concerning <u>Jeremiah</u> (We've seen he is a type of the Man-child.) **to Nebuzaradan the captain of the guard, saying, (12) Take him, and look well to him, and do him no harm; <u>but do unto him even as he shall say unto thee</u>.** Now wouldn't you like that to happen to you during a time when the beast is seeking to destroy the rebellious people of God? **(13) So Nebuzaradan the captain of the guard sent, and Nebushazban, Rab-saris, and Nergal-sharezer, Rab-mag, and all the chief officers of the king of Babylon, (14) they sent, and took Jeremiah out of the court of the guard, and committed him unto Gedaliah the son of Ahikam, the son of Shaphan, that he should carry him home: so he dwelt among the people.** Oh, praise God! Why did Joseph, Daniel, Jeremiah, etc. have favor with the king? They prophesied, interpreted, or spoke the <u>truth</u> concerning God's people. The king felt that Jeremiah was on his side because Jeremiah was telling those apostate Jews that, "God is the One Who raised up this beast kingdom to come against you because you are in rebellion to his Word. You are not eating the Lamb and you are not vaccinated from the judgments that are going to come from this kingdom against you." Yet here we find somebody who has been vaccinated. Here we find that Jeremiah and those who listened to him, those who submitted and humbled themselves to God, escaped judgment. I'm sure it impressed the king to find out that God was speaking judgments through Jeremiah that the king, himself, was going to be bringing to pass on the very same people. It's very interesting how the people of the world, and even the beast, are more impressed with God's prophecies when they come to pass than God's people are.

Let's go back to Jeremiah 21 one final time. ***(Jer.21:7) And afterward, saith the Lord, I will deliver Zedekiah king of Judah, and his servants, and the people, even such as are left in this city from the pestilence, from the sword, and from the famine, into the hand of Nebuchadrezzar king of Babylon, and into the hand of their enemies, and into the hand of those that seek their life: and he shall smite them with the edge of the sword; <u>he shall not spare them</u>, <u>neither have pity</u>, <u>nor have mercy</u>.*** It can be hard to understand why so many of God's people are going to die in these days, but God is against our flesh, our carnal man. He's not against our spirit man. Our spirit man has been persecuted by the carnal man, brought into bondage by the carnal man, just as it was in Egypt. The Egyptians, who represent the carnal man, brought the Israelites, who represent the spiritual man, into bondage. The Israelites had to go through a "baptism" in the Red Sea to get rid of the carnal man, to drown the Egyptian, so that the spiritual man, the Israelite, would be free (1 Corinthians 10:2).

God's not in favor of our spiritual man being in bondage to our carnal man, ruled over by our carnal man. The man of flesh is against God; he is anti-Christ. Jesus said, ***(Luk.17:33) Whosoever shall seek to gain his life shall lose it: but whosoever shall lose [his life] shall preserve it.*** We <u>have</u> to lose our life in order to gain our life and this old man ruling in our life has to be put to death. For that reason, the Bible speaks a lot about God's people going through death in the Tribulation. Of course, if they are God's people, then by putting them to death physically God is setting them free from that old man who rules their life. When we get baptized, we accept by <u>faith</u> the death of the old man. We accept by <u>faith</u> that we were crucified with Christ. ***(Gal.2:20) I have been crucified with Christ; and it is no longer I that live, but Christ living in me: and that [life] which I now live in the flesh I live in faith, [the faith] which is in the Son of God, who loved me, and gave himself up for me.*** It's no longer us who live, but it's Christ Who lives in us and we accept it by faith. Are you willing to see this manifested? Are you willing to see the death, burial, and resurrection of Jesus manifested in you? Are you willing to go that far? You can't have much of the self life with the old man dead, and if He has to do it, God will cut off the physical life to get rid of the self life.

Folks, we're coming to a time when the overwhelming majority of God's people have been living just like we read here in Jeremiah 19, 20, and 21. They have a "Jesus" of their own making and so they're not believing in the true Jesus of the Bible. ***(Joh.7:38) He that believeth on me, <u>as the scripture hath said</u>...*** Their "Jesus" is not "as the scripture hath said" and that means they're not assimilating the Word into their life and into their actions. Jesus is not foolish. He knows who loves Him. ***(Joh.14:15) If ye love me, <u>ye will keep my commandments</u>... (23) ... If a man love me, <u>he will keep my word</u>: and my Father will love him, and we will come unto him, and make our abode with him.*** There are many times when a person has repented but the spiritual man is too weak to overcome the carnal man. Yes, they want God. Yes, they want freedom from their bondage, yet they can't find their way to freedom. They're blinded by the god of this world because their flesh is stronger than they are. It takes eating the Word of God to get our eyes opened to see Who He is and what He wants. It takes eating the Word of God to learn what it is to abide in Jesus Christ, which is to walk as He walked (1 John 2:6). That's how we identify the true body of Christ.

Choosing Self-Willed Rebellion Vs. Death to Self

Many of God's people will have to enter the Kingdom through physical death; they will not go there any other way. It's better to die by the Sword of the Spirit, which is the Word of God (Ephesians 6:17), than to die by the sword of this world. Dead men don't have to die because they're not under the curse, and we're here to put the old man to death. We're here to walk in the light of God's Word, which is our "water" baptism, and to let that water put to death the old man. Otherwise, God may have to bring the enemy in like a flood (Daniel 11:10; Isaiah 59:19). Instead, we can choose to accept the "flood" of our baptism, we can walk in repentance and faith, we can devour the Word of God, and we can see Jesus, on Whom there is no curse, <u>manifested</u> in us. Or we can walk in stubborn, self-willed rebellion, giving in to our old man, repenting at the last minute by the Grace of God and having to lose our physical life in order to enter the Kingdom. God is merciful and He loves us. **(Mic.7:18) Who is a God like unto thee, that pardoneth iniquity, and passeth over the transgression of the remnant of his heritage? he retaineth not his anger for ever, because he delighteth in lovingkindness.** He'll do what's necessary to bring us in.

Choose to Walk In Holiness

I'm sad to say that there will be a great falling away of people who will never enter in, because they have given in to the flesh and God is not granting them repentance (2 Thessalonians 2:3). It's like the story of Esau (Hebrews 12:16), but we are coming to the end now, the time when God said, **(Rev.3:15) I know thy works, that thou art neither cold nor hot: I would thou wert cold or hot. (16) So because thou art lukewarm, and neither hot nor cold, <u>I will spew thee out of my mouth</u>.** Of course, we would rather be "hot" because "cold" is death. He doesn't want to judge "lukewarm" fence-riders, either, so we're coming to the time when God has to do something to very quickly bring us into the Kingdom. I know that many people will repent when they see what their life has brought them to; they will repent, and God will love and save them. He will bring them into the Kingdom, and that's great, but wouldn't you rather eat the Lamb so that you can escape the judgments that are coming from the king of Babylon? Wouldn't you rather escape dying by the sword or dying by the guillotine or dying by the plagues? Wouldn't you rather escape all the different judgments that are going to be sent out against God's people in the days to come? I would rather walk holy before the Lord and be like Jeremiah, because **(Pro.16:7) When a man's ways please the Lord, He maketh even his <u>enemies</u> to be at peace with him.** Notice Jeremiah had his provision given to him by the hand of the enemy; the enemy was even giving fields and so forth to these poor of the land. Those of them who stayed with Jeremiah didn't go into captivity. The type and the shadow is there. Jesus and His disciples didn't go into captivity, even though they were in a land of captivity. They were free and they were the only ones there who were free. **(Joh.8:36) If therefore the Son shall make you free, ye shall be free indeed.**

There are many angry and unforgiving people who will demand their own way and they will fight. They will be like Barabbas (Mark 15:7; Luke 23:19); they will fight in order to keep their rights. Christians who love the Lord and want to serve Him don't care where they go to share the Word of God. It's not important to them to have the things of the world. They're not worried about their rights, they're more concerned about serving God. They're more interested in seeing their brethren come into the Kingdom. There are so many out there who call themselves "Christian" yet they want to fight to get "their nation" back; they don't understand that's just fighting for <u>this</u> world. They want to fight instead of just obeying the Sermon on the Mount (Matthew chapter 5; Luke 6:20-42) and taking every opportunity to serve the Lord and build <u>His</u> Kingdom. They want to see the return of the worldly kingdom that they once had. Well, the Lord is not interested in that and I tell people, "You know, you will <u>never</u> take America back; it's not going to happen."

Disqualifications for Christ's Passover

When this world becomes the Kingdom of our Lord and of His Christ, <u>then</u> we will get the land back (Revelation 11:15). Until then, it's going to go downhill all the way because God is raising-up an enemy to our <u>enemy</u>; He's raising-up an enemy to the <u>flesh</u>.

God raised-up both the Roman Empire beast and the people of Israel to crucify the body of Christ (Acts 2:22-24, 4:1-31), exactly as was prophesied. **(Zec.13:7) Awake, O sword, against my shepherd, and against the man that is my fellow, saith the Lord of hosts: <u>smite the shepherd</u> and the sheep will be scattered <u>and I will turn my hand upon the little ones</u>.** The Lord took out the Master through the beast, through the harlot, through wicked men. He crucified the body of Christ back then and now He's getting ready to do it in our day. Folks, Jesus was set <u>free</u> at the Cross! He was set free to walk in the Kingdom of His Father. We have a choice. We can bear our spiritual cross, a death to self, or we can go to our more physical cross, a death to that fleshly body, to which we've submitted and by which we've been ruled over. There is a choice. In the days to come, I would rather be in the first-fruits Man-child, as we saw in Jeremiah, or among those disciples who follow him and serve the Lord with gladness. As Jesus told us, **(Mat.6:31) Be not therefore anxious, saying, What shall we eat? or, What shall we drink? or, Wherewithal shall we be clothed? (32) For after all these things do the Gentiles seek; for your heavenly Father knoweth that ye have need of all these things. (33) <u>But seek ye first his kingdom, and his righteousness; and all these things shall be added unto you</u>.** His disciples lived a simple lifestyle, not caring for the things of the world, serving the

Lord in truth and in purity. I would rather be there because that's where we have God's vaccination, His provision, His deliverance, His redemption from our enemies.

(Luk.1:68) Blessed be the Lord, the God of Israel; For he hath visited and wrought redemption for his people, (69) And hath raised up a horn of salvation for us In the house of <u>his servant David</u>. Of course, that was Jesus in that day. In our day, the son of David is a body of reformer ministers in whom Jesus lives, called the "Firstfruits." **(70) (As he spake by the mouth of his holy prophets that have been from of old), (71) <u>Salvation from our enemies</u>, <u>and from the hand of all that hate us</u>...** Wow! Jesus provided this total salvation. Remember the Bible says, **(Pro.16:7) When a man's ways please the Lord, He maketh even his enemies to be at peace with him.** And we can see those types and shadows: Joseph was preserved; Daniel was preserved; Jeremiah was preserved. The difference between them as types of the Man-child and Jesus as the Man-child, is that their crucifixion was the death of the old man. They went through a spiritual crucifixion and died to self, but Jesus was physically crucified; His flesh was crucified as a sacrifice for us all. As representatives of God, these men went through much persecution and crucifixion to become leaders of God's people. So, did God provide them salvation from their enemies and salvation from all the people that hated them? He certainly did! Joseph was delivered from prison, Daniel from the lions' den, Jeremiah from the apostate leadership. You may ask, "Well, if that's the case, David, why do we see the beast conquering the people of God in Revelation 13?" The beast is conquering those people because they are not willing to go through the death of their old man without his help, but if a person cooperates in the daily crucifixion process, then Revelation 13 may not be necessary for them.

The Time to Repent is Now!

(Luk.1:71) Salvation from our enemies, and from the hand of all that hate us; (72) To show mercy towards our fathers, And to remember his holy covenant; (73) The oath which he spake unto Abraham our father (74) To grant unto us that we being delivered out of the hand of our enemies Should serve him without fear (75) In holiness and righteousness before him all of our days. Well, we've seen that salvation and deliverance came to some, but not to all, because all weren't getting inoculated. They waited until it was too late. We know that our Passover Lamb is our inoculation and we know we have to eat all of the Lamb. If you <u>are</u> eating the Lamb, you can put the Blood over the doorposts so that the destroyer passes over when he comes to smite the Egyptians. We have a Passover, but few know it, although it's clearly in the Word of God, and that Passover is not for everybody; it's only for those who have eaten the Lamb. Praise be to God! We've also seen that eating the "unleavened bread" is the same as eating the "Lamb" because Jesus was the Word made flesh. He's called the "Word of God," the *logos* (John 1:1,14). The unleavened bread is not leavened by what man adds to make the flesh accept it. We don't need the religious leaven of the Pharisees of another "Jesus"; we don't need the secular leaven of Herod of worshiping and serving worldly kingdoms. We want no leaven in our bread. We need the unleavened bread. The Lord warned us that anybody who had leaven in their houses for those last seven days before they left Egypt, "that soul shall be cut off from Israel" (Exodus 12:15,19). We must partake of only unleavened bread, only the pure Word of God, and we will be vaccinated. Glory be to God!

CHAPTER THREE

Abiding in the Secret Place of the Most High

Father, we thank You in the Name of Jesus, for working in our hearts the life of Your Son. We thank You for all Your vast provision that's even over and above all we could ask or think. We thank You for Your provision for the whole man, Lord. We do pray, Lord, that You would reveal this to all of Your elect children. Reveal to them, Lord, that we do have the provision of Your holy manna. We thank You, Father, that we can trust in You. You are our "vaccination" in times when man-made and devil-made diseases are flying rampant everywhere; You're our Savior, You're our Provider. You created our Passover Lamb. You gave us the victory through Him, and we accept that gift of God. Lord, we thank You that "There shall no plague to be upon you to destroy you," as your Word in Exodus 12 tells us. We praise You for that and for Your promise, "I will put none of the diseases upon thee, that I have put upon the Egyptians: for I am the Lord that healeth thee" in Exodus 15. We thank You for that, for Your full provision, Lord. We know that we have a better Covenant, based on better promises, while so many of Your people don't know that we have a better Covenant. Thank You, Lord, for the revelation of God covering the earth as the waters of the sea. Thank You, Lord, that Your people in these days will come to know You fully. Hallelujah!

In our last chapter, we discovered those who aren't going to be prepared for the plagues that are coming upon this world, and we also found out that God is the One sending those plagues. We learned that He will use the plagues to take out the wicked and, in the texts that we studied, we saw that He was going to use those plagues to take out the wicked among His people, also. Now I'd like for us to encourage ourselves a little because the Bible says, **(Col.4:6) <u>Let your speech be always with grace</u>, seasoned with salt, that ye may know how ye ought to answer each one.** And I thought Psalm 91 would be a perfect place to start since it does mention judgments such as pestilences and plagues, and how the Lord has delivered us from all of that if we'll just believe it. It's the Word of God.

The Psalm 91 Passover

(Psa.91:1) He that dwelleth in the <u>secret place</u> of the Most High... Of course, that's the first thing people want to know: "David, where is this 'secret place of the Most High'?" Well, He just told you in the text. It says, "in the secret place of the Most High." <u>He</u> is the "secret place." As Moses said, **(Psa.90:1) Lord, <u>thou</u> hast been our dwelling-place in all generations.** The Lord Christ, Himself, is the secret place where we abide. It's completely unknown to the world and sadly, unknown even to most of God's people, but if we understand what abiding in Christ is, we will understand the secret place. We're told, **(1Jn.2:5) But whoso keepeth his word, in him verily hath the love of God been perfected. Hereby we know that we are in him: (6) he that saith he abideth in him ought himself also to walk even as he walked.** Jesus told the disciples, **(Joh.14:12) Verily, verily, I say unto you, <u>he that believeth on me</u>, <u>the works that I do shall he do also</u>; and greater works than these shall he do; because I go unto the Father.** That's the life of a Christian, and we don't have any right to describe it otherwise. The one who believes on Him is the one who, as He said, does "the works that I do" because *(Jas.2:17) ...faith, if it have not <u>works</u>, is dead in itself.* When we have faith, the works that are manifested through us are not our works; they're <u>God's</u> works, and that's what a lot of people don't understand.

When you believe in God's Word, God's Word empowers you, because the Gospel "is the power of God unto salvation to everyone that believeth." *(Rom.1:16) For I am not ashamed of the gospel: for it is the power of God unto salvation to every one that <u>believeth</u>; to the Jew first, and also to the Greek.* So who gets "the power of God"? It's only the "one that <u>believeth</u>." If a person doesn't have power, then they're not believing "as the scripture hath said." *(Joh.7:38) He that believeth on me, <u>as the scripture hath said</u>, from within him shall flow rivers of living water. (39) But this spake he of the Spirit, which they that believed on him were to receive: for the Spirit was not yet given; because Jesus was not yet glorified.* We want to be found believing on Him "as the scripture hath said," because this is abiding in Christ. The Lord is narrowing it down for us here, *(Mat.22:14) For many are called, but few chosen.* We see it once again as we read on. *(1Jn.2:24) As for you, let that abide in you which ye heard from the <u>beginning</u>.* (In other words, it's not some modern-day religion or doctrine or church government or whatever. It's only this Word that came down out of heaven that gives life unto the world {Joh.6:33}.) *If that which ye heard from the beginning abide in you, ye also shall abide in the Son, and in the Father.*

So if the Word abides in you, then you have the Truth living in you and that's what it is to totally abide in the Son. "He that <u>dwelleth</u> in the secret place of the Most High," is <u>abiding</u> in God.

(1Jn.3:6) <u>***Whosoever abideth in him sinneth not***</u>***: whosoever sinneth hath not seen him, neither knoweth him.*** The one in you that doesn't sin is your spiritual man, the one that is born from above. The one in you that does sin is the carnal man, the one that is born from beneath, and that carnal man has no part in the Kingdom of Heaven. We have to lose our life in this world to gain our life (Matthew 16:25; Mark 8:35; Luke 17:33; John 12:25). That Life we gain is Jesus Christ, the Word of God, growing in us 30-, 60-, and 100-fold, so that we may be that fruit that He comes and picks. He's not coming to pick the plant; He's coming to pick the fruit. He doesn't want the plant because the plant is your old, corrupt life that has grown up out of the dirt of this earth. ***(1Jn.4:16) And we know and have believed the love which God hath in us. God is love; and*** <u>***he that abideth in love abideth in God***</u>***, and God abideth in him.*** "He that abideth in love abideth in God," because "God is love."

So we see that there are some conditions to abiding in the secret place of the Most High. You may be worrying, "David, that's making it kind of hard for us to be protected." No, it's really not hard. The people who think it's hard are the people who are not believing on Him "as the scripture hath said." When we believe only what the Word of God says and nothing else, no religious spirit, no false religion, no false doctrines, then we base our life on that. And when we're seeking to come into conformity to the Word, of course, we get the power of God that we need because the Gospel is *(Rom.1:16) ... the power of God unto salvation to every one that believeth...* You will bear fruit in every area of your life where you are believing those words from God.

You can waste your whole life in religion, folks, but as the Bible says, only the Word of God manifested in you is going to enter the Kingdom. *(Joh.3:13) And no one hath ascended into heaven, but he that descended out of heaven, even the Son of man, who is in heaven.* In the Parable of the Sower, Jesus as the Sower went forth and sowed the seed, and the seed was the Word of God that went into hearts to bring forth fruit, 30-, 60-, and 100-fold. *(Mat.13:18) Hear then ye the parable of the sower. (19) When any one heareth the word of the kingdom, and understandeth it not, then cometh the evil one , and snatcheth away that which hath been sown in his heart. This is he that was sown by the way side. (20) And he that was sown upon the rocky places, this is he that heareth the word, and straightway with joy receiveth it; (21) yet hath he not root in himself, but endureth for a while; and when tribulation or persecution ariseth because of the word, straightway he stumbleth. (22) And he that was sown among the thorns, this is he that heareth the word; and the care of the world, and the deceitfulness of riches, choke the word, and he becometh unfruitful. (23) And he that was sown upon the good ground, this is he that heareth the word, and understandeth it; who verily beareth fruit, and bringeth forth, some a hundredfold, some sixty, some thirty.* It's the Word that brings forth the "fruit," and the "fruit" is Christ, Himself. *(Col.1:27)*

... ***Christ in you, the hope of glory.*** This is what God is after.

If we abide in Him, we have His provision, His protection, but that's not the case if you are walking in sin and rebellion against Him. ***(Jas.4:17) To him therefore that knoweth to do good, and doeth it not, to him it is sin.*** With knowledge, comes responsibility. In the New Testament, sin is attributed to you when you know to do good, yet you don't do it. ***(Heb.10:26) For if we sin wilfully after that we have received the knowledge of the truth, there remaineth no more a sacrifice for sins, (27) but a certain fearful expectation of judgment, and a fierceness of fire which shall devour the adversaries.*** When we know what God wants us to do and we believe in His Word, God will empower us to walk in that Word. This is not us picking ourselves up by our bootstraps; this is God doing the work in us. We're trusting in Him to be and to do what He said He would do. It's not us coming into conformity by our own ability, it's Him bringing us into His conformity by His ability. Our faith in Him is what does that.

Walking In New Light Each Day

Are you walking in that faith? Are you walking in Light? ***(1Jn.1:6) If we say that we have fellowship with him and walk in the darkness, we lie, and do not the truth: (7) but if we walk in the light, as he is in the light, we have fellowship one with another, and the blood of Jesus his Son cleanseth us from all sin.*** It doesn't say, "stand in the light," it says, "walk in the light," because when you walk in the light, you are continuing to walk in new light, more and more light, every moment. Now you don't know the light that's at the other end of the road. You've never been there, but God's not holding you accountable for that light, and that's the great thing about the New Covenant. **(Jas.4:17) To him therefore that <u>knoweth</u> to do good, and doeth it not, to him it is sin.** It's not as hard as you might think, because all that God wants you to do is <u>walk</u> in what you <u>know</u>. He wants you to continue to learn more and more so that you may bear more and more fruit. Of course, there are a lot of people who deceive themselves. They just put the Bible to the side and since they aren't learning anything, they think they're not accountable for anything. Well, what happens then is that you don't bear fruit. And if you don't bear fruit, you don't enter the Kingdom, because the fruit is the fruit of the seed of the Word of God. That's the seed that bears fruit in your heart, according to the Parable of the Sower.

(Psa.91:1) He that dwelleth in the secret place of the Most High Shall abide under the shadow of the Almighty. There's your protection, your blessing, your provision. Notice this is somebody who is walking with the Lord and seeking to be pleasing unto Him. They're <u>holding fast</u> to the faith of the Gospel. Sure, they fail, but they confess their sins and they're forgiven, and they get back up and continue to exercise faith in those promises. The Bible says that the Lord considers them to be righteous because of their faith alone. **(Rom.4:5) But to him that worketh not, but believeth on him that justifieth the ungodly, his <u>faith is reckoned for righteousness</u>.** Faith is another thing that puts us in Christ. We are accounted as righteous through our faith because **(Heb.11:1KJV) ... faith is the substance of things**

hoped for, the evidence of things not seen. We are to receive what God says is ours by faith. Maybe you haven't seen it manifested in your life yet, but you should receive it by faith because God says it's yours. And because you believe and are righteous, God will manifest your answer in the physical realm. This is all part of "walking in the light," which is abiding in the "secret place of the <u>Most High</u>," Who is <u>God</u>. If you're doing your own thing and going your own way, you can't expect God to give you the provision or not to chasten you for your rebellion. If God would keep on blessing a person who continues in their rebellion, He would be like a bad parent who doesn't chasten their child. Of course, you're going to raise a spoiled brat that way. God doesn't do that. If you are truly a child of God, He's going to chasten you when you turn aside from His way (Isaiah 65:2; Jeremiah 6:16; Romans 3:12; etc.)

Here's another text about "the secret place of the Most High" that uses a slightly different wording. ***(Psa.32:7)*** <u>***Thou art my hiding-place***</u>***; thou wilt preserve me from trouble…*** We hide in God. When we abide in Him, we are hidden from trouble, and you can count on that. I'd like to backup and look at more of the text because it's very important. ***(Psa.32:1) Blessed is he whose transgression is forgiven, Whose sin is <u>covered</u>.*** Obviously, this is speaking about being covered by the Blood. He's accounted righteous because he has confessed his sins and he's walking by faith. That's what the text talks about, confessing your sins. ***(2) Blessed is the man unto whom the Lord <u>imputeth not iniquity</u>*** (Again, God doesn't count his sins against him because he's confessed them and he's walking by faith, and faith is accounted as righteousness.)***, And in whose spirit there is no <u>guile</u>.*** You see, many people are just lying to themselves. They want to justify themselves. They don't want the Word of God, like a two-edged sword, to put their old life to death. They don't want to let the waters of the Word of God, in their baptism, put their old life to death. They are full of guile and deception. They've made-up ear-tickling doctrines that permit them to believe they're okay as they are, instead of being honest enough to confess their sins so that God will forgive them and deliver them.

Let the Word Transform You

(Psa.32:3) When I kept <u>silence</u> (In other words, "While I didn't deal with my sin."), ***my bones wasted away Through my groaning all the day long. (4) For day and night <u>thy hand was heavy upon me</u>…*** The chastening of the Lord is upon those who continue in their sins, who don't deal with them, but ***(1Jn.1:9) If we confess our sins, he is faithful and righteous to forgive us our sins, and to cleanse us from all unrighteousness.*** We need to come to Him, confess the sin, and walk by faith in the promises so that we don't continue in the sin. Some people confess the sin, and they confess the sin, and they confess the sin, and yet there's no repentance there. Repentance means that there is a <u>change</u> of mind. The Bible says, ***(2Co.7:10) For godly sorrow worketh repentance unto salvation, a repentance which bringeth no regret: <u>but the sorrow of the world worketh death</u>.*** "The sorrow of the world" doesn't change anybody; the person just keeps going back to what they were. "Godly sorrow worketh repentance," which is a change of mind. If you have "a change of mind," that's "a renewing" of your mind. We're told, ***(Rom.12:2) And be not fashioned according to this world: but <u>be ye transformed by the renewing of your mind</u>, and ye may prove what is the good and acceptable and perfect will of God.*** Of course, when you renew your mind with the Word, you're going to be transformed.

(Psa.32:4) For day and night thy hand was heavy upon me: My moisture was changed as with the drought of summer. Selah. Your life comes from your bones because that's where your blood is created. The Bible speaks quite often about how your bones are dried up when you walk in sin (Psalm 102:3; Proverbs 17:22; Lamentations 4:8; Ezekiel 37:11; etc.) ***(Psa.32:5) I acknowledged my sin unto thee, And mine iniquity did I not hide: I said, I will confess my transgressions unto the Lord; And thou forgavest the iniquity of my sin. (6) For this let every one that is godly pray unto thee <u>in a time when thou mayest be found</u>*** (Many, many will wait until it's too late, until judgment comes upon them for their sins.)***: Surely <u>when the great waters overflow</u> they shall not reach unto him.*** There's judgment coming, folks, and the way to escape it is to confess your sins so that you will be accounted as righteous before the Lord and to repent, because this is how you come to be abiding in Him. ***(7) Thou art my hiding-place; thou wilt preserve me from trouble; Thou wilt compass me about with songs of deliverance. Selah.*** Notice the faith involved here, the confession that's involved here. He's not <u>asking</u> God for this, he's proclaiming that he <u>has</u> it, on the grounds of God's Word. "Thou art my hiding-place." "Thou wilt preserve me from trouble." "Thou wilt compass me about with songs of deliverance." Praise God! So once more, "abiding in Christ" is confessing any sins, accepting your righteousness in Christ, and reckoning **(Rom.6:11) ... *ye also yourselves to be dead unto sin*, but alive unto God in Christ Jesus.**

Many people don't understand how to get rid of their sin, to not just confess it. But as we've seen, you reckon yourself to be "dead unto sin, but alive unto God" (Romans 6:11) by what Jesus did at the Cross. **(Rom.6:6) Knowing this, that *our old man was crucified with him*, *that the body of sin might be done away*, that so we should no longer be in bondage to sin; (7) for he that hath *died is justified from sin*.** If you're dead, then sin has no more power over you. **(Rom.6:18) And *being made free from sin*, ye became servants of righteousness. (22) But now being *made free from sin* and become servants to God, ye have your fruit unto sanctification, and the end eternal life.** You were made free from sin by the sacrifice of Jesus Christ. That brings the imputation of righteousness unto you and the power that you need to walk away from the sin in the first place.

God Grants Repentance by His Grace

Returning to Psalm 91, we can see the same thing. **(Psa.91:1) He that dwelleth in the secret place of the Most High Shall abide under the shadow of the Almighty. (2) *I will say of the Lord*, He is my refuge and my fortress; My God, in whom I trust.** You know, it's not enough to have faith; faith without works is dead (James 2:14,17). You have to act on your faith in some way, and the most common way is to speak your faith.

(Rom.10:10) With the heart man believeth unto righteousness; and with the mouth confession is made unto salvation. Jesus promised, *(Mat.10:32) Every one therefore who shall confess me before men, him will I also confess before my Father who is in heaven.* The Greek word there translated "confess" is *homologeó* and it means simply to "speak the same as." What does God say about you? Well, He says that you're a new creature. *(2Co.5:17) Wherefore if any man is in Christ, he is a new creature: the old things are passed away; behold, they are become new.* He says you're born from above. *(Joh.3:3) ... Verily, verily, I say unto thee, Except one be born anew, he cannot see the kingdom of God.* He says you're made free from sin. *(Rom.6:18) And being made free from sin, ye became servants of righteousness. (22) But now being made free from sin and become servants to God, ye have your fruit unto sanctification, and the end eternal life.* He says you're dead to sin. *(Rom.6:11) Even so reckon ye also yourselves to be dead unto sin, but alive unto God in Christ Jesus.* God says these things. We're only repeating what He says. When we say of the Lord, "He is my refuge," we're confessing, "I do abide in Christ, not by my own power, but by His power. He drew me. He granted me repentance." Many people think they can choose to repent, but God grants us the gift of faith and the gift of repentance. Jesus told us, *(Joh.15:16) Ye did not choose me, but I chose you, and appointed you, that ye should go and bear fruit, and that your fruit should abide: that whatsoever ye shall ask of the Father in my name, he may give it you.*

(Psa.91:2) I will <u>say</u> of the Lord, He is my refuge and my fortress; My God, in whom I trust. When is the best time to say this? We should constantly be saying that we're abiding in Christ, but especially when there's a threat. Are you going to agree with God then, or are you going to agree with your fears, your doubts, all these things that assail you? Here's the same confession repeated a little further down. *(9) For thou, O Lord, art my <u>refuge</u>! Thou hast made the Most High thy habitation.* We confess that the Lord is our refuge, but most of God's people don't believe that. They don't believe that there's even any provision made for the natural man. They don't believe that there is safety in Him, as all of Psalm 91 says. Some pastors actually preach in their churches that this is for the Millennium (Revelation 20:1-5). Well, then this promise won't do them any good, because they're unbelievers in that regard.

Praise is a Confession of His Promises

(Psa.91:2) I will say of the Lord, He is my refuge and my fortress; my God, in whom I trust. Oh, praise be to God! Many people don't understand that <u>praise is a confession</u> to the Lord. It's a confession in His promises. Psalm 149 is also an awesome revelation of this. The Hebrew word for "praise" there is *hallel,* which means "to boast or to brag on" what the Lord has done. What did God do? Stop and think about it: He saved you; He delivered you; He made you holy; He made you free from sin; He provided <u>everything</u> for you. He <u>did</u> all these things, as the Scripture declares. In fact, any problem you have was taken care of by the Lord, on the Cross. When we praise

God, we're bragging that these things are done. We're doing what Jesus told us to do when He said, *(Mar.11:24)* ***... All things whatsoever ye pray and ask for, believe that ye <u>received</u> them, and ye shall have them.*** We believe we have received, *(Rom.10:10) **for with <u>the heart man believeth</u> unto righteousness; and with <u>the mouth confession is made</u> unto salvation.*** We believe we have received and we prove it by what we <u>say</u>, by what we <u>do</u>, by how we <u>act</u>. When we believe we have received, we're going to receive it; that's what Jesus said. It's going to be manifested. Now we can understand that ***(Psa.149:6) Let the high praises of God be in their mouth...*** is talking about a confession of what God has already done for you. It is speaking your faith, and ***(Heb.11:1KJV) ... <u>faith is the substance</u> of things hoped for, the evidence of things not seen.*** That "substance" is what God uses to bring the manifestation, the material thing, to pass. Whatever the provision is that you need, you give God the substance and He gives you the manifestation, because ***(Mat.10:32) Every one therefore who shall confess me before men, him will I also confess before my Father who is in heaven.***

(Psa.149:6) Let the high praises of God be in their mouth, And a <u>two-edged sword</u> in their hand. The "two-edged sword," of course, is the Word. ***(Heb.4:12) For the <u>word of God is living</u>, and active, <u>and sharper than any two-edged sword</u>, and piercing even to the dividing of soul and spirit, of both joints and marrow, and quick to discern the thoughts and intents of the heart.*** The Word of God is not in your physical hand, it's in the hand of your spiritual man. ***(Eph.6:17) And take the helmet of salvation,***

and the <u>sword of the Spirit</u>, <u>which is the word of God</u>. There are many people who can quote the Word of God, but it doesn't do them any good. However, when the spiritual man has the Word of God, believes on the Word of God, and speaks the Word of God, that's powerful. Many people pervert the Word of God because, even though they can quote it perfectly, they don't understand what it says and so they don't apply it rightly.

(Mat.10:28) And be not afraid of them that kill the body, but are not able to kill the soul: but rather fear him who is able to destroy both soul and body in hell. We are not to fear man. Fear is the very opposite of faith, it is the opposite of our confession. Fear is destructive. Any fear that you have amounts to faith in the negative, faith in the curse, faith in the devil. Jesus says to not fear any man, but fear the Lord, "who is able to destroy both soul and body in hell." *(Mat.10:29) Are not two sparrows sold for a penny? and not one of them shall fall on the ground without your Father* (In other words, the Lord has complete care over all of His creation.)*: (30) but the very hairs of your head are all numbered. (31) Fear not therefore: ye are of more value than many sparrows. (32) Every one therefore who shall confess me before men, him will I also confess before my Father who is in heaven.* Jesus is the Apostle and High Priest of our confession (Hebrews 3:1), and He tells us, *(Mat.18:18) Verily I say unto you, what things soever ye shall bind on earth shall be bound in heaven; and what things soever ye shall loose on earth shall be loosed in heaven.* So as you can see, our confession is very important.

As we confess Jesus Christ, confess Him before men, "speak the same as" before men, then our High Priest takes that offering and offers it before the Father. That's how we receive what we receive from God. ***(Mat.10:33) But whosoever shall <u>deny</u> me before men, him will I also deny before my Father who is in heaven.*** Quite often, when we make that mistake, it is because we are being tempted to pay more attention to what we see in this <u>world</u> rather than what we see in the <u>Word of God</u>. We're not ***(2Co.10:5) casting down imaginations, and every high thing that is exalted against the knowledge of God, and bringing every thought into captivity to the obedience of Christ.*** Instead, we're casting down the Word of God; we're giving-up the Word in the midst of a fiery trial, and when we do that, we don't continue to confess the Lord. We have to put on our armor. We have to swing our Sword. We have to diligently put the Word of God into our hearts and then He can bring it to our remembrance to defend us against whatever situation we're facing in this world (John 14:26), whether it's the curse, the devil, the flesh, whatever. <u>We</u> have to confess Him before men so that <u>He</u> can confess us before the Father.

(Psa.149:6) Let the <u>high praises of God</u> be in their mouth, And a two-edged sword in their hand; (7) To execute vengeance upon the nations... Remember what happened when three armies came against Jehoshaphat and he put the praisers out front to confess the Lord before men. ***(2Ch.20:21) And when he had taken counsel with the people, he appointed them that should sing unto the Lord, and <u>give praise in holy array</u>, as they went out <u>before</u> the army, and say, Give thanks unto the Lord; for his loving-***

kindness endureth for ever. (22) And when they began to sing and to <u>praise</u>, the Lord set liers-in-wait against the children of Ammon, Moab, and mount Seir, that were come against Judah; and they were smitten. (23) For the children of Ammon and Moab stood up against the inhabitants of mount Seir, utterly to slay and destroy them: and when they had made an end of the inhabitants of Seir, <u>every one helped to destroy another</u>. The enemies destroyed each other because, when the praisers began to praise and confess God, then the Lord Jesus was able to confess them before God and they received an awesome deliverance.

(Psa.149:7) To execute vengeance upon the nations, And punishments upon the peoples; (8) To bind their <u>kings</u> with chains, And their <u>nobles</u> with fetters of iron. I don't doubt that a lot of people think that this is only talking about physical kings, but I believe that there are also spiritual kings, principalities and powers, who rule over the natural kings and the flesh and so on and so forth. A good example is where Isaiah speaks about the "king" of Babylon. *(Isa.14:4) That thou shalt take up this parable against the <u>king of Babylon</u>, and say, How hath the oppressor ceased! the golden city ceased! (5) The Lord hath broken the staff of the wicked, the scepter of the rulers; (6) that smote the peoples in wrath with a continual stroke, that ruled the nations in anger, with a persecution that none restrained. (7) The whole earth is at rest, and is quiet: they break forth into singing.* As he continues to talk along that vein, we find this. *(12) How art thou fallen from heaven, O <u>day-star</u>,*

son of the morning! (Now this is speaking of Lucifer. The Hebrew word there for "day-star" is *helel* and it means "lucifer--a shining one.") ***How art thou cut down to the ground, that didst lay low the nations! (13) And thou saidst in thy heart, I will ascend into heaven, I will exalt my throne above the stars of God; and I will sit upon the mount of congregation, in the uttermost parts of the north; (14) I will ascend above the heights of the clouds; I will make myself like the Most High.*** Most people recognize that as Satan, and yet, now he's also being called the "king of Babylon." Well, we know that there's a natural king of Babylon, but Babylon was the "head" of the nations. Babylon represented the head of gold (Daniel 2:32), which ruled over a body which was made up of all world-ruling nations beneath that head (Daniel 2:31-45). Folks, Satan has taken over the "head." This is the mind of the beast (Daniel 4:16, Daniel chapter 7; Revelation chapter 13). Satan's mind is the mind of the beast and he's ruling the world. He's the god of this world and he's ruling the body through the head.

So we see that Psalm 149 is talking about the saints having authority over the "kings," both spiritual and physical. ***(Psa.149:8) To bind their kings with chains, And their nobles with fetters of iron; (9) To execute upon them the judgment written: This honor have **all his saints**. Praise ye the Lord.*** Notice that's "all his saints," from even the least to the greatest. His saints, with the two-edged sword in their hand and with the high praises of God in their mouth, have authority over the principalities, the powers, and the rulers. We have that authority, not to do our will, but to do God's Will (Luke 22:42; John 5:30, 6:38). We're here to do the Father's Will, and the Lord uses His body here in the earth. Just as He used the body of Jesus Christ 2,000 years ago to exercise His authority, He uses the body of Christ today to exercise His authority. Jesus said that the Father gave Him authority because He was a son of man, not because He was the Son of God. ***(Joh.5:26) For as the Father hath life in himself, even so gave he to the Son also to have life in himself: (27) and <u>he gave him authority to execute judgment</u>, <u>because he is a son of man</u>.*** God gave Him authority in the earth because He was a son of man. When God gave that authority to Adam, Adam lost it because he sinned. Jesus, the last Adam, didn't sin and therefore, He retained His authority. He passed it on to His children, His disciples. He passed on that authority to <u>us</u>. ***(Mat.18:18) Verily I say unto you, what things soever ye shall bind on earth shall be bound in heaven; and what things soever ye shall loose on earth shall be loosed in heaven.***

<u>We have authority</u> to speak things that will bring destruction to the enemy and that will bring protection to us, just as the high praises of God did for Jehoshaphat's army. The Bible says, ***(Psa.50:14) Offer unto God the sacrifice of thanksgiving; And pay thy vows unto the Most High: (15) And call upon me in the day of trouble; <u>I will deliver thee</u>, <u>and thou shalt glorify me</u>. (Psa.50:23) Whoso offereth the sacrifice of thanksgiving glorifieth me; And to him that ordereth his way aright <u>Will I show the salvation of God</u>.*** And, ***(Psa.54:6) With a freewill-offering will I sacrifice unto thee: I will give thanks unto thy name, O Lord, for it is good. (7) For <u>he hath delivered me out of all trouble</u>***... He <u>has</u> delivered us "out

of <u>all</u> trouble." We've been made free from the curse of this world by the sacrifice of Jesus Christ. Of course, we will live under a curse when we need chastening for our sins because we haven't repented and confessed them quickly enough, and so we've come under judgment. In that case, we receive chastening but we don't have to stay there. We can walk by faith in Jesus Christ. We can confess our sins. We can get back up and believe that He took away our sins. We can believe that "He hath delivered me out of all trouble." Jesus became a curse for us that we might have Abraham's blessings. ***(Gal.3:13) Christ redeemed us from the curse of the law, having become a curse for us; for it is written, Cursed is every one that hangeth on a tree: (14) that upon the Gentiles might come the blessing of Abraham in Christ Jesus; that we might receive the promise of the Spirit through faith.***

He <u>has</u> delivered us from all trouble, according to His Word, which is what Psalm 91 is all about: "<u>My God</u>, <u>in whom I trust</u>." ***(Psa.91:3) For he will deliver thee from the snare of the fowler…*** "He <u>will</u> deliver thee" is not a "maybe." If you're "in the secret place of the Most High" because you've repented and confessed your sins before Him, then you're abiding in Christ to the best of your ability. Then you're walking in the light that you know, and He will deliver you. ***(Psa.91:3) For he will deliver thee from the snare of the fowler, And from the deadly pestilence.*** The apostle Timothy speaks about the snare of the devil and being taken captive by him to his will. ***(2Ti.2:25) In meekness correcting them that <u>oppose themselves</u>*** (Sinners "oppose themselves." They do what is destructive to them. They need to repent, they need to change their mind, to turn and go the other way.)

if peradventure God may give them repentance unto the <u>knowledge of the truth</u>, (Of course, if you know the truth, the truth will set you free {John 8:32}.) ***(26) and they may recover themselves out of the snare of the devil, having been taken captive by him unto <u>that will</u>.*** Your Bible translation may say "his will" there, however, the numeric pattern shows that the correct translation is "that will." Some people are taken captive by the devil and they serve him. They are taken captive by him, and are taken captive by his will, but they can recover themselves if they will repent, because in repentance, there is provision from God, protection from God.

(2Ti.3:10) But thou didst follow my teaching, conduct, purpose, faith, longsuffering, love, patience... You know, we have been given Jesus Christ to show us what we're supposed to look like. ***(2Co.3:18) But we all, with unveiled face beholding as in a mirror the glory of the Lord, <u>are transformed into the same image</u> from glory to glory, even as from the Lord the Spirit.*** So Who is our "idol"? It's the Lord, Himself. We want to come into His Image. The Bible says, ***(1Jn.3:3) And every one that hath this hope [set] on him purifieth himself, even as he is pure.*** We desire earnestly to walk in His steps, and we've been given examples such as Paul, who said, ***(1Co.11:1) Be ye imitators of me, even as I also am of Christ.*** In other words, "Follow me, as I follow the Lord." We don't want to follow people who don't follow the Lord. ***(2Ti.3:10) But thou didst follow my teaching, conduct, purpose, faith, longsuffering, love, patience, (11) persecutions, sufferings. What things befell me at Antioch, at Iconium, at Lystra; what persecutions I***

*endured. **And out of them all the Lord delivered me.*** Praise be to God!

The Lord Will Deliver Me From Every Evil Work

Some people are not convinced that the Lord wants to deliver them "out of them all." If the devil can convince you that, "You need to keep this curse" or "You need to keep that curse," then you will, because that's where your faith is. Jesus said to the centurion, ***(Mat.8:13) ... Go thy way; as thou hast believed, [so] be it done unto thee...*** And as Jesus said to the two blind men, ***(Mat.9:29) ... According to your faith be it done unto you.*** It's all according to how you believe. If, like the apostle Paul, you believe that God will deliver you "out of them all," then God will do that for you, too. ***(2Ti.4:18) The Lord will deliver me from every evil work...*** "The Lord will deliver me": there's the confession, there's the praise that binds the kings, that confounds the enemy, that causes the enemy to destroy themselves. How could Paul say that? If you're thinking, "Oh, because he's Paul." No, it doesn't have anything to do with that. God is not a respecter of persons (Acts 10:34-35). Paul also said ***(1Co.9:27) but I buffet my body, and bring it into bondage: lest by any means, after that I have preached to others, I myself should be rejected.*** Even after he had preached to others, he said that, so, no, he's not a special person. He is still someone who has to walk in the secret place of the Most High. ***(2Ti.4:18) The Lord will deliver me from every evil work, and will save me unto his heavenly kingdom: to whom be the glory forever and ever. Amen.*** Yes, "to whom be the glory," because it has nothing to do with us, it has to do with what God promised <u>He would do</u> if we would just believe. He didn't make it hard, He just wants us to believe.

(Psa.34:17) The righteous cried, and the Lord heard, And <u>delivered</u> them out of all their troubles. (18) The Lord is nigh unto them that are of a broken heart, And <u>saveth</u> such as are of a contrite spirit. (19) Many are the afflictions of the righteous; But the Lord <u>delivereth</u> him out of them all. If you don't believe there's an end to your trial, if you don't believe there is a deliverance from the curse of sickness and so on and so forth, then, of course, you can't have it even though Jesus gave it to us at the Cross. Psalm 91 is a wonderful promise of God's provision to protect us, to save us, to deliver us. Praise God! ***(Psa.91:3) For he will deliver thee from the snare of the fowler, <u>And from the deadly pestilence</u>.*** Back when this was written, there were no vaccinations available, but God's Power is made perfect in our weakness (2 Corinthians 12:9). The less we put in, the more God puts in. That's the way it works. Some people have found that they're actually made sick by vaccines, but still, those vaccines are the best that man knows to do. Folks, there is nothing that can deliver man from the curse but faith in Jesus Christ, <u>nothing</u>. ***(Jer.17:5) Thus saith the Lord: <u>Cursed is the man that trusteth in man</u>, and maketh flesh his arm, and whose heart departeth from the Lord.*** There's always a curse in man's provision. There's always a curse in man's efforts to deliver you from the curse. There's always a curse in man's efforts to deliver you from the just penalty of your sin. Without faith in Jesus Christ, there really isn't any way that deliverance can happen.

You can put your trust in the vaccines of this world, but ultimately, they're going to fail along with everything else. Or, you can put your trust in the Lord and in His promises, because His provisions will be perfect, and you won't have to put up with all the terrible side-effects of man's meddling with nature. ***(Psa.91:3) For he will deliver thee from the snare of the fowler, And from the deadly pestilence.*** Praise be to God! ***(4) He will cover thee with his pinions*** (He's saying that you're back under the shadow of the Almighty.)***, And under his wings shalt thou take refuge: <u>His truth</u> is a shield and a buckler.*** Notice that He covers you with His pinions, you're under His wings, and His truth is your shield and buckler. In other words, you are protected by His truth, and His truth is what? His truth is the "wings"! You're under His wings, you're protected by His wings, His truth. You know that the truth will set you free (John 8:32). The truth is also what gives us the power to live above the world. The phrase "wings of the eagle," many times in the Scriptures, is applied to the overcomer. He has given us the power to fly above this world, in heavenly places, in Christ, where we have our provision. ***(Eph.1:3) Blessed be the God and Father of our Lord Jesus Christ, who hath blessed us with every spiritual blessing in the <u>heavenly places in Christ</u>.*** We're able to fly above this world because we believe the truth. It's not only a protection, it's a provision to be able to overcome and fly above the danger. There's not much that can hurt an eagle as long as he's flying in the air, but when he comes to the earth, it's very dangerous. He can lose his life there.

(Psa.91:5) <u>Thou shalt not be afraid</u> for the terror by night, Nor for the arrow that flieth by day. "I shall not be afraid." We have to be reminded of that quite often. It's very dangerous to walk in fear since the provision that God gave us is a provision that is manifested only through our faith, and faith is the very opposite of fear. Whenever you have fear, you should treat it as a spirit of fear attacking you because that's what it is. You should fight with it, you should cast it down. Fear is one of the devil's big guns. Whenever you are doing something by <u>faith</u> in God, the devil sends fear against you. He usually fires thoughts into your mind, and if you give heed to those thoughts, fear will start taking over. You'll notice that fear usually comes when you begin to think negatively, when you begin to think on things that are contrary to the promise, but when you cast down those vain imaginations, fear has no power whatsoever (2 Corinthians 10:5). Fear comes when your emotions get stirred-up because you choose to believe something other than the promise of God, or when your heart condemns you because you're walking in sin.

God Has Complete Provision for Those Who Fear Not

(Php.4:19) And my God shall supply <u>every need</u> of yours according to his riches in glory in Christ Jesus. You see, God made <u>complete</u> provision for us, but we can't take advantage of it unless we have faith, and it's hard to have faith without a clean conscience, so confess your sins. **(1Jn.3:21) Beloved, <u>if our heart condemn us not</u>, we have boldness toward God; (22) and whatsoever we ask we receive of him, because we keep his commandments and do the things that are pleasing in his sight.** Also, if we want to be bold in our faith, we have to be **(2Co.10:5) casting down imaginations, and every high thing that is exalted**

against the knowledge of God, and bringing every thought into captivity to the obedience of Christ. We have to cast down fear. Whenever you are stepping out by faith, you can expect the devil to show up with his spirits of fear, but fear can never take hold if you don't believe what he says. Cast down what he says and you will not fear. If you believe what he says, he'll take you over and that's when you will fail to receive God's provision, God's protection. You may have to go through a trial of your faith like this before you receive, but ***(Heb.10:23) let us hold fast the confession of our hope that it waver not; for he is faithful that promised.***

(Psa.91:5) Thou shalt not be afraid for the terror by night, Nor for the arrow that flieth by day; (6) For the <u>pestilence</u> that walketh in darkness… The reason that God's people "absorb" these things is because they're fearful. They don't <u>believe</u> in the promise of God, they're not <u>standing</u> on the promise of God, they're not <u>confessing</u> the promise of God, they're not <u>praising</u> the promise of God. In the very early 1900s, John G. Lake was a missionary to South Africa during an outbreak of the Bubonic Plague and he never caught the disease. He explained it, "Fear absorbs every curse and faith repels it." He believed, he had faith, in the provision of God.

Testimony: John G. Lake During the Bubonic Plague

Now watch the action of the law of life. Faith belongs to the law of life. Faith is the very opposite of fear. Faith has the opposite effect in spirit, and soul, and body. Faith causes the spirit of man to become confident. It causes the mind of man to become restful, and positive. A positive mind repels disease. Consequently, the emanation of the Spirit destroys disease germs.

And because we were in contact with the Spirit of life, I and a little Dutch fellow with me went out and buried many of the people who had died from the bubonic plague. We went into the homes and carried them out, dug the graves and put them in. Sometimes we would put three or four in one grave.

We never took the disease. Why? Because of the knowledge that the law of life in Christ Jesus protects us. That law was working. Because of the fact that a man by that action of his will, puts himself purposely in contact with God, faith takes possession of his heart, and the condition of his nature is changed. Instead of being fearful, he is full of faith. Instead of being absorbent and drawing everything to himself, his spirit repels sickness and disease. The Spirit of Christ Jesus flows through the whole being, and emanates through the hands, the heart, and from every pore of the body.

During that great plague that I mentioned, they sent a government ship with supplies and corps of doctors. One of the doctors sent for me, and said, "What have you been using to protect yourself? Our corps has this preventative and that, which we use as protection, but we concluded that if a man could stay on the ground as you have and keep ministering to the sick and burying the dead, you must have a secret. What is it?"

I answered, "Brother, that is the 'law of the Spirit of life in Christ Jesus.' I believe that just as long as I keep my soul in contact with the living God so that His Spirit is flowing into my soul and body, that no germ will ever attach itself to me, for the Spirit of God will kill it." He asked, "Don't you think that you had better use our preventatives?" I replied, "No, but doctor, I think that you would like to experiment with me. If you will go over to one of these dead people and take the foam that comes out of their lungs after death, then put it under the microscope, you will see masses of living germs. You will find they are alive until a reasonable time after a man is dead. You can fill my hand with them and I will keep it under the microscope, and instead of these germs remaining alive, they will die instantly." They tried it and found it was true. They questioned, "What is that?" I replied, "That is 'the law of the Spirit of life in Christ Jesus.' When a man's spirit and a man's body are filled with the blessed presence of God, it oozes out of the pores of your flesh and kills the germs."

Suppose, on the other hand, my soul had been under the law of death, and I were in fear and darkness? The very opposite would have been the result. The result would have been that my body would have absorbed the germs, these would have generated disease and I would have died.

You who are sick, put yourself in contact with God's law of life. Read His Word with the view of enlightening your heart so that you will be able to look up with more confidence and believe Him. Pray that the Spirit of God will come into your soul, take possession of your body, and its power will make you well. That is the exercise of the law of the Spirit of life in Christ Jesus.

(Rom.8:2) For the law of the Spirit of life in Christ Jesus made me free from the law of sin and of death. (Luk.10:19) Behold, I have given you authority to tread upon serpents and scorpions, and over all the power of the enemy: and nothing shall in any wise hurt you.

CHAPTER FOUR

Believe the Truth and Be Set Free!

Father, in the Name of Jesus, we thank You for being our God. Thank You that You have chosen us and are drawing us to Yourself to reveal Your Son in us. Thank You, Lord, that You are our protection, our Passover, our Psalm 91 "secret place." Teach us to abide in You, Lord, through faith in Your Word, through repentance, through turning away from the world. Thank You so much, Father, that You're teaching us how to think, how to speak, and how to be justified in our words in the coming time of judgment, as the apostle Paul said, so that we might prevail. We thank You, Father, that You "vaccinate" Your saints against the plagues that are coming upon this world. You said that "neither shall any plague come nigh thy tent," and so we thank You for Your vaccination, Lord. We don't trust the world's vaccination, but we trust in You, Father. Thank You so much! Amen!

We've been studying Psalm 91, and I'd like to back up to where the Lord says that ***(Psa.91:4) He will cover thee with his pinions, And under his wings shalt thou take refuge: His <u>truth</u> is a shield and a buckler.*** We pointed out from this text that being hidden under God's "wings" means you're being hidden under His truth, and also, it's by His truth that we overcome the world. ***(Joh.8:31) Jesus therefore said to those Jews that had <u>believed</u> him, If ye abide in my word, [then] are ye truly my disciples; (32) and ye shall know the truth, and <u>the truth shall make you free</u>.*** The truth, the wings, set you free from the law of gravity, from being bound to the world. God's truth is what causes us to be able to walk in the Spirit and overcome the world. Truth, according to this verse, is necessary for God's protection. It's His shield, it's His buckler.

The story of Hosea has a lot to say about truth. The name "Hosea" means "Salvation" and comes from a root word that means "Deliverer," so we can see who he represents there, and in a type and shadow for history, God had Hosea marry Gomer, a harlot. Gomer's name actually means, "completion" or "to finish." The neat thing about it is, Gomer represents just exactly that: the complete harlot family of God, from the beginning to this day. The Scripture teaches that there is a body called the "Harlot," but when the "Savior" was married to this harlot, she brought forth three children, and I would like to talk to you about the last two, a daughter called "Lo-ruhamah," which means "That hath not obtained mercy," and a son called "Lo-ammi," which means, "Not my people." God likened Lo-ruhamah to the house of Israel (Hosea 1:6), and then, after Lo-ruhamah was weaned, they had Lo-ammi. These are pretty negative names for anybody to be naming their children, but they represented a body of people that God wanted to save, so God encouraged them to speak to one another, leaving off the word, "Lo," which is the Hebrew for "not."

(Hos.2:1) Say ye unto your brethren, <u>Ammi</u> (No longer Lo-ammi, "not my people," but "my people."**), and to your sisters, <u>Ruhamah</u>.** No longer Lo-ruhamah, "that hath not obtained mercy," but "that hath obtained mercy." Here, according to His Word, they were beginning to <u>confess faith</u> for one another here. I believe quite firmly that these two represented Israel and the Gentile church, and we're going to see that it bears out in Scripture. One thing God says to these two children is that their mother, Gomer the harlot, is not his wife. *(2) Contend with your mother, contend; for she is not my wife, neither am I her husband; and let her put away her whoredoms from her face, and her adulteries from between her breasts; (3) lest I strip her naked, and set her as in the day that she was born, and make her as a wilderness, and set her like a dry land, and slay her with thirst. (4) Yeah, upon her children will I have no mercy; for they are children of whoredom; (5) for their mother hath played the harlot...* Think about it, folks. Israel and the church both have brought forth a child of whoredom. Both have gone astray from God. Both have been taken captive to the harlot of Babylon.

(Hos.2:14) Therefore, behold, I will allure her, and bring her into the wilderness, and speak comfortably unto her. (15) And I will give her her vineyards from thence, and the valley of <u>Achor</u> ("Achor" means "troubling.") *for a door of hope; and she shall make answer there, <u>as in the days of her youth</u>...* She is going to turn back to the Lord. He's going to bring her through "troubling" and He is going to turn her back to the Lord in the wilderness. Obviously, that doesn't mean everyone, but it does represent a remnant, which the Lord calls "Ruhamah" and "Ammi," that will turn back to the Lord. Toward the end of this chapter, He speaks to them again. *(Hos.2:23) And I will sow her unto me in the earth; and I will have mercy upon her <u>that had not obtained mercy</u>* (That's Lo-ruhammah; "not" is the "Lo."); *and I will say to them that were <u>not my people</u>*, (That's Lo-ammi.), *Thou art my people; and they shall say, [Thou art] my God.* The Lord is saying that

He is going to save a people <u>out</u> of both of these groups, Israel and the church.

Is all of what we call the "church" going to be saved? No. Is all of natural Israel going to be saved? No. Only a remnant out of the church and a remnant out of natural Israel will be saved. They will be joined together into one body **(Rom.11:26) and so <u>all Israel</u> shall be saved...** Notice in that chapter, it's both those Gentiles who were grafted-in and those who were faithful in Israel, that are now called "all Israel." **(Rom.11:23) And they also, if they continue not in their unbelief, shall be grafted in: for God is able to graft them in again. (24) For if thou wast cut out of that which is by nature a wild olive tree, and wast grafted contrary to nature into a good olive tree; how much more shall these, which are the natural [branches], be grafted into their own olive tree?** In these days, the Lord is going to bring in a faithful remnant of the Church and a faithful remnant of Israel. They're going to become "one new man." **(Eph.2:14) For he is our peace, who made both one, and brake down the middle wall of partition, (15) having abolished in the flesh the enmity, [even] the law of commandments [contained] in ordinances; that he might create in himself of the two <u>one new man</u>, [so] making peace; (16) and might reconcile them both in one body unto God through the cross, having slain the enmity thereby.** It's not that the Lord hasn't already done that. He paid for that at the Cross, and it's going to be fulfilled and finished in our day.

Then a new parable starts about another woman, whom I believe represents these two, joined together, and it speaks about how he's going to save these two. ***(Hos.3:1) And the Lord said unto me, Go again, love a woman beloved of [her] friend, and an adulteress...*** This is the second symbolic marriage of Hosea. The first symbolic marriage was the Harlot, and the second symbolic marriage, I believe, is a prophecy of the New Covenant, because in the New Covenant, God did join together both Israel and the Gentiles through faith in Jesus Christ. ***(Hos.3:1) And the Lord said unto me, Go again, love a woman beloved of [her] friend, and an adulteress, even as the Lord loveth the children of Israel, though they turn unto other gods, and love <u>cakes of raisins</u>.*** Cakes of raisins are shriveled-up, small and sometimes old, fruit that's been pressed together, which as a spiritual type, speaks badly of their nature since they loved this.

(Hos.3:2) So I bought her to me for fifteen [pieces] of silver, and a homer of barley, and a half-homer of barley; (3) and I said unto her, Thou shalt abide for me many days; thou shalt not play the harlot, and thou shalt not be any man's wife: so will I also be toward thee. (4) For the children of Israel shall abide many days <u>without</u> a king, and <u>without</u> prince, and <u>without</u> sacrifice, and <u>without</u> pillar, and <u>without</u> ephod or teraphim. Now we know that's been literally true of natural Israel, and spiritually true of spiritual Israel, because they've been in captivity in Babylon. Of course, natural Israel was in bondage to Babylon and Assyria and all the other world-ruling entities. Then we see this revelation of a great restoration to come. ***(Hos.3:5) Afterward shall the children of Israel return, and seek the Lord their God and David their king, and shall come with fear unto the***

Lord and to his goodness <u>in the latter days</u>. So this second symbolic marriage ends-up with a remnant of both Israel and the Church coming to the Lord in the latter days.

Two chapters later, the Lord speaks again of leaving them, which actually happened in history 2,000 years ago. *(Hos.5:15) I will go and return to my place, till they acknowledge their offence, and seek my face: in their affliction they will seek me earnestly.* The reason for tribulation is to cause God's people to seek Him diligently. In the coming affliction, they are going to return. In the letter, this is speaking about Israel, but spiritually speaking, the Church is spiritual Israel (Romans 2:28-29) and what's true in the letter is also true in the Spirit. A prophecy is first fulfilled naturally, in the letter, but the second time it's fulfilled, most often it's fulfilled spiritually.

(Hos.6:1) Come, and let us <u>return</u> unto the Lord... "Return" from where? God's people were being encouraged to return from their Babylonish captivity. That's exactly what was happening here, just as in Hosea chapter 3 they were returning, and in the end of Hosea chapter 2 they were returning. He took away their prefix, "Lo," which is "not," and He called them those "that hath obtained mercy" and "my people." *(Hos.6:1) Come, and let us return unto the Lord; for he hath torn, and he will heal us; he hath smitten, and he will bind us up. (2) After two days will he revive us: on the third day he will raise us up, and we shall live before him. (3) And let us know, let us follow on to know the Lord: his going forth is sure as the morning; and he will come unto us as the rain, as the latter rain that watereth the earth.* On the "morning" of the "third day," the Lord is going to come and use the "latter

rain" to restore His people. The latter rain is going to bring about this joining of spiritual Israel with natural Israel, which is going to come into the Kingdom and also become spiritual Israel. The way that God joins natural Israel to spiritual Israel is that they must be born again. There's no other way to enter the Kingdom. No other covenant does God accept, despite what the reprobate preachers out there say. The truth is that you have to be born again. That's what Jesus said you must do to enter the Kingdom (John 3:3,5-6). He's not accepting any other covenant, contrary to some of the false doctrine out there, and now that we understand that, we can understand whom chapter 4 is speaking to. Remember that we are talking about how important truth is to the preservation of God's people. It's His shield and His buckler. It is that with which He protects His people. It is His pinions, it is His wings, under which we can hide.

(Hos.4:1) Hear the word of the Lord, ye children of Israel; for the Lord hath a controversy with the inhabitants of the land, because there is no truth, nor goodness, nor <u>knowledge of God</u> in the land. Of course, it's the knowledge of the truth that's going to protect God's people in these days. **(Psa.91:4) He will cover thee with his pinions, And under his wings shalt thou take refuge: His <u>truth</u> is a shield and a buckler.** God's people are going to be destroyed for lack of knowledge. Many people are going to lose their lives physically, and some spiritually, because of their lack of knowledge. **(Hos.4:2) There is nought but swearing and breaking faith, and killing, and stealing, and committing adultery; they break out, and the blood toucheth blood. (3) Therefore shall the land mourn, and every one that dwelleth therein shall**

languish, with the beasts of the field and the birds of the heavens; yea, the fishes of the sea also shall be taken away. (4) Yet let no man strive, neither let any man reprove; for thy people are as they that strive with the priest. (5) And thou shalt stumble in the day, and the prophet also shall stumble with thee in the night; and I will destroy thy <u>mother</u>. God is speaking about Gomer. There are many people who are called "Christians" but they're members of the Harlot; they've never "come out" of her and God warns, *(Rev.18:4) And I heard another voice from heaven, saying, <u>Come forth</u>, <u>my people</u>, <u>out of her</u>, that ye have no fellowship with her sins, and <u>that ye receive not of her plagues</u>: (5) for her sins have reached even unto heaven, and God hath remembered her iniquities.*

(Hos.4:6) <u>My</u> people... Far too many people think that they can never be lost because they claim to be His people and they had a born again experience in their spirit. They think that they can never be destroyed. They think that the judgment of God would not come upon them, but the Bible says otherwise. *(Hos.4:6) <u>My people are destroyed for lack of knowledge</u>: because thou hast rejected knowledge, <u>I will also reject thee</u>...* Wow! If <u>you</u> desert truth, <u>you</u> will be deserted. That's what the Lord is saying here. He will reject you if you reject knowledge. Many people do want to follow after their ear-tickling false gods because of selfish ambition, and they ignore God's Word. We need to seek God's Will alone and reject anything having to do with Christianity that's man-made, or else, in the time of trouble, God says He will reject you. *(Hos.4:6) My people are destroyed for lack of knowledge:*

because thou hast rejected knowledge, I will also reject thee, that <u>thou shalt be no priest to me</u>: seeing that thou has forgotten the law of thy God, I also will forget thy children. If we're not a priest to the Lord, that's a serious offense.

(Exo.19:4) Ye have seen what I did unto the Egyptians, and how <u>I bare you on eagles' wings, and brought you unto myself</u>. Those "eagles' wings" were how God's people escaped Egypt, and they're how the "woman" escapes the beast in Revelation. *(Rev.12:14) And there were given to the woman the two wings of the great eagle, that she might fly into the wilderness unto her place, where she is nourished for a time, and times, and half a time, from the face of the serpent.* Revelation speaks of the repetition of history. "I bare you on eagles' wings, and brought you unto myself." These "wings" are the truth (Psalm 91:4) that God gives us that causes us to overcome the world, to live above the world, to live in the Spirit rather than to be subject to the curses that are upon this earth.

(Exo.19:5) Now therefore, if ye will obey my voice indeed... God still puts a high premium on obedience today; it's just that we come at obedience from a different direction, and that is grace. We receive the grace from God to be obedient because of our faith in His promises. Praise be to God! That's awesome! To say that God doesn't need you to be obedient is a lie that's being taught in many religions. They don't understand that the power to obey comes by grace from God. *(Exo.19:5) Now therefore, if ye will obey my voice indeed, and keep my covenant, then ye shall be <u>mine own possession from among all peoples</u>; for all the earth is mine*

(That's what we want to be, not only the called, but the <u>chosen</u>. We want to be His "own possession from among all peoples," the remnant from among all peoples that God is calling together.)***: (6) and ye shall be unto me a <u>kingdom of priests</u>...*** These chosen people, this chosen remnant, is going to be a "kingdom of priests." If He rejects you from being a priest because you have rejected knowledge, then you are completely rejected because <u>all</u> of His remnant are priests. ***(Exo.19:6) And ye shall be unto me a <u>kingdom of priests</u>, and a <u>holy nation</u>...*** If you are a New Testament priest of the Lord, then you offer up sacrifices unto the Lord, and the "flesh of beasts" that you offer is the flesh of your own "beast." ***(Rom.12:1) I beseech you therefore, brethren, by the mercies of God, to <u>present your bodies a living sacrifice</u>, holy, acceptable to God, [which is] your spiritual service.*** We present our bodies as a living sacrifice to God by serving Him. If you do that, you are a part of His holy nation. If you don't do that, you are not. It doesn't matter that you've gone to some church and shaken a preacher's hand and "received Jesus as your personal Savior"; you're still not a member of His holy nation. ***(Exo.19:6) And ye shall be unto me a kingdom of priests, and a holy nation. These are the words which thou shalt speak unto the children of Israel.*** Amen!

(Hosea 4:6) My people are destroyed for lack of knowledge: because thou hast rejected knowledge, I will also reject thee, that thou shalt be no priest to me: seeing thou hast forgotten the law of thy God, I also will forget thy children. So if you reject knowledge, He will reject you from being a priest, and if you are rejected from being a priest, you are rejected from being a part of His holy nation. "Holiness" is being separated from the world unto God. The truth is given to us to separate us from the world, and the people who <u>obey</u> the truth are <u>manifesting</u> their sanctification from the world. That's why God sends His truth. That's why He renews our minds. **(Rom.12:2) And be not fashioned according to this world: but <u>be ye transformed by the renewing of your mind</u>, and ye may prove what is the good and acceptable and perfect will of God.** What renews our mind? <u>Truth</u>. **(Pro.8:17) I love them that love me; And those that seek me diligently shall find me. (18) Riches and honor are with me; [Yea,] durable wealth and righteousness. (19) My fruit is better than gold, yea, than fine gold; And my revenue than choice silver. (20) I walk in the way of righteousness, In the midst of the paths of justice; (21) That I may cause those that love me to inherit substance, And that I may fill their treasuries.** When we love truth and seek after truth as choice silver, God gives it to us, and it does separate us. This renewing of our mind transforms us from a worldly person into a spiritual person, from being a son of the world to being a son of the Father.

(Hos.4:7) As they were multiplied, so they sinned against me: I will change their glory into shame. (8) They feed on the sin of my people, and set their heart on their iniquity. (9) And it shall be, like people, like priest; and I will punish them for their ways, and I will requite them their doings. There will be no grace for those people who forsake the offer of grace. In these days, God is separating the wheat from the tares. Wheat and tares may look very much alike as they grow, but tares bring forth only tiny, very useless fruit. God's going to separate them because He's going to pick only His true fruit, 30-, 60-, and 100-fold (Matthew 13:23; Mark 4:13-20; Luke 8:8). **(Hos.4:10) *And they shall eat, and not have enough; they shall play the harlot, and shall not increase; because they have left off taking heed to the Lord.*** So they rejected knowledge and they're going to find no help, no grace, no power in the days to come, until they change their mind. I suspect that by bringing His people into the valley of "Achor," or "troubling," that some of these people are going to repent and become a faithful remnant. They may have been "Lo-ruhamah" and "Lo-ammi," but they'll now be "Ruhamah" and "Ammi." **(Hos.4:11) *Whoredom and wine and new wine take away the understanding.*** "Whoredom" is receiving the "seed" of the world, receiving the doctrines and ideas of man. Jesus sowed the only Seed that will bring forth fruit of Christ, and that is the Seed of the Word of God. There is nothing that can form Christ in us but the Word of God. Anything else is whoredom.

(Hos.4:12) *My people ask counsel at their stock, and their staff declareth unto them; for the spirit of whoredom hath caused them to err, and they have played the harlot, [departing] from under their God.* Only the people who love truth so much that they won't depart from it, are going to be protected. Psalm 91 is for them. Psalm 91 is not for what we loosely call the "church." They have been playing the harlot, but those people who love the truth and won't depart from it, will be protected. They are under His "wings." They have His "shield and buckler." **(Psa.91:5) <u>Thou shalt not be afraid</u> *for the terror by night, Nor for the ar-***

row that flieth by day... We are told, ***(Psa.23:4) Yea, though I walk through the valley of the shadow of death, I will fear no evil; for thou art with me...*** That was a psalm of David, a man who was after God's Own heart (Acts 13:22). If we are after God's heart, if we love His truth, if we want to be obedient to Him, God is going to be our help. If we live to be seen of Him and not to be seen of men, if we are, as priests, sacrificing our old fleshly, beastly self on the altar of trials, troubles, and tribulations, God is going to be our help. If we're forsaking the world and we're loving sanctification, God is going to be our help. You know, if a person has fear in the midst of the "shadow of death," it's usually because they don't really love God. Jesus said, ***(Joh.14:15) If ye love me, ye will keep my commandments.*** And, ***(Joh.14:23) ... If a man love me, he will keep my word: and my Father will love him, and we will come unto him, and make our abode with him.*** That's a person who loves the truth and so they're protected.

We're headed, at this particular point, towards the most dangerous times in history. Wouldn't you like God to keep you in faith and boldness and fearlessness through this time? Well, if you seek Him with all of your heart, He will do that. He will protect your mind. You will have on the helmet of salvation, which is the knowledge that you've been saved from all of these fearful things that are coming upon the world. He tells us to "fear not" (Isaiah 54:4; Matthew 10:28; Luke 12:4; etc.) He tells us, "though I walk through the valley of the shadow of death, I will fear no evil; for thou art with me." A person who is confident that the Lord is with them is fearless. ***(Isa.54:14) In righteousness shalt thou be established: thou shalt be***

far from oppression, for thou shalt not fear; and from terror, for it shall not come near thee. Does everybody have that confidence? No, and many people will lose it at the last moment, either because they're in idolatry with a false god they're calling "Jesus," or because their heart condemns them, so they don't really believe that God is on their side. ***(1Pe.3:6) As Sarah obeyed Abraham, calling him lord: whose children ye now are, if ye do well, and are <u>not put in fear by any terror</u>.*** Fear comes to <u>separate</u> you from God. ***(1Jn.4:18) There is no fear in love: but perfect love casteth out fear, because fear hath punishment; and <u>he that feareth is not made perfect in love</u>.*** The person that fears is the person who believes what the curse says, believes what the devil says, believes in the threat that they see with their eyes, whether it be in darkness or in light. Their fear is the very opposite of faith.

Faith is believing in the preservation that the Lord has given to us in Psalm 91, and fear is believing that you are under the curse and that it will take you out when it comes through. The person who is full of faith and is hidden under God's truth, will be sheltered under the wings of the Lord when these terrible plagues come through. We know that some of the plagues that are mentioned in Exodus are not actually diseases. They're other kinds of judgments upon Egypt, but God's people, God's truly devoted people, are going to be protected from them, too. Some people think having fear is normal and don't really think of fear as being sin. Well, what does the Bible say? ***(Rev.21:8) But for the <u>fearful</u>, and <u>unbelieving</u>*** (Look at that! These two lead this list.)***, and abominable, and murderers, and fornicators*** (We don't generally put the fearful and unbelieving in the same category as murderers and fornicators, do we?), **and sorcerers, and idolaters, and all liars, their part [shall be] in the lake that burneth with fire and brimstone; which is the second death.** Folks, being fearful and in unbelief is offensive to God; it is a <u>sin</u>. It is a sin that's ranked with these other sins and it's one that will separate you from God forever.

We need to fill our hearts with truth. **(Rom.10:17) So <u>belief</u>** (This is the Greek word *pistis* meaning "faith, belief, trust.") **[cometh] of hearing, and hearing by the word of Christ.** The *King James* translates this, **So then faith [cometh] by hearing, and hearing by the word of God.** You need <u>His</u> faith, you need the faith that God has. Praying in the Holy Spirit is another way to increase your faith. **(Jud.1:20) But ye, beloved, building up yourselves on your most holy faith, praying in the Holy Spirit...** But the main way that you receive faith is through loving the truth, seeking the truth, putting the truth into your heart until it becomes a part of your heart and a part of your vocabulary. **(Rom.10:10) For with the heart man believeth unto righteousness; and with the mouth confession is made unto salvation.**

In the midst of the fiery trial, when you are threatened by the curses and plagues of the world, will you confess Him then? That's the whole point. Will you confess His promise then? Will you confess that Psalm 91 is yours? Will you confess that you are hidden in the secret place of the Most High? Your <u>confession</u>, in the trial, is the only way that salvation can be made complete. Faith without works is dead. **(Jas.2:17) Even so faith, if it have not works, is dead in itself.** You can <u>say</u> that you believe, but <u>during</u>

the trial that comes to see if you believe, your actions need to match your words. You need to be "walking your talk," because that's what's going to protect you from the curse of this world. God will supernaturally send forth His protection for you if you will confess Him in the midst of the trial. ***(Psa.91:11) For he will give his angels charge over thee, To keep thee in all thy ways.*** When the plague is all around you, can you say, "A thousand shall fall at my side, And ten thousand at my right hand; But it shall not come nigh me"? Can you say that because you know that you are seeking after God and your heart is not condemning you? Can you confess, "It shall not come nigh me," because you believe it? You need to know that you can do that <u>now</u>. In the trials you are in <u>now</u>, cast down fear and doubt and ***(Heb.10:23) ... hold fast the confession of*** (your) ***hope that it waver not; for he is faithful that promised.***

 (Heb.2:14) Since then the children are sharers in flesh and blood, he also himself in like manner partook of the <u>same</u> (That is, the same flesh and blood.)***; that through death he might bring to nought him that had the power of death, that is, the devil.*** By His death, Jesus brought to nothing the power of the devil. This is to <u>deliver</u> us from all fear, even though the overwhelming majority of Christianity does not believe this. They don't care what the Bible says; they don't believe that Jesus died in order to actually <u>deliver</u> us from any kind of fear, including the fear of death. If your conscience is clear, you can have bold faith in God and you can believe His promises. Make sure that you're in right standing with the Lord, that you've confessed, repented of, and forsaken your sins. True repentance means you've had a change of mind and you are no longer going to run after those things, you're no longer going to live in the lusts of your flesh but are going to serve God. True repentance means with the heart you are believing in His promises, believing that you are delivered from these sins and from these curses. And true repentance means that with the mouth you're going to confess it.

So now you can also confess that your God will protect you because the curse of death is upon sinners, but you have forsaken your sins and come to God and trust in Him, even if you're not perfect. That's what the Blood Covering is all about. **(Heb.2:14) Since then the children are sharers in flesh and blood, he also himself in like manner partook of the same; that through death he might bring to nought him that had the power of death, that is, the devil; (15) <u>and might deliver all them who through fear of death were all their lifetime subject to bondage</u>.** What puts people in bondage is the fear of death. That fear forces them to do things that are totally contrary to faith in God. They're in bondage to those things because they fear death, yet, the Lord came to <u>deliver</u> us from the fear of death. We are free from the fear of death because of the sacrifice of Jesus.

(Heb.3:14) For we are become partakers of Christ, if we hold fast the beginning of our confidence firm unto the end: (15) while it is said, Today <u>if ye shall hear his voice</u>, Harden not your hearts, as in the provocation. Do you hear His Voice? Do your brethren tell you of His Voice? Do they tell you of His promises, of the things that His Word says? And are you humbling yourself to His Word, or are you hardening your heart because you have ulterior motives and want to do your own thing? He's warning you here. **(Heb.3:16)**

For who, when they heard, did provoke? Nay, did not all they that came out of Egypt by Moses? (17) And with whom was he displeased forty years? was it not with them that sinned, whose bodies fell in the wilderness? They were murmuring and complaining. They were not speaking the Word of God. They didn't believe His promise of their provision and of His protection. ***(Num.14:2) And all the children of Israel murmured against Moses and against Aaron: and the whole congregation said unto them, Would that we had died in the land of Egypt! or would that we had died in this wilderness!*** Well, God told Moses, ***(Num.14:28) Say unto them, As I live, saith the Lord, surely as ye have spoken in mine ears, so will I do to you: (29) your dead bodies shall fall in this wilderness...*** So they died because they <u>refused to believe</u> His Word. They didn't enter into His rest. ***(Heb.3:18) And to whom sware he that they should not enter into his rest, but to them that were <u>disobedient</u>?*** The Greek word there is *apeitheó*, which means "I disobey" or, literally, "I refuse to be persuaded." It comes from the word *apeithea* meaning "willful unbelief." It's obvious that if you are unbelieving, you will be disobedient, because obedience comes from <u>belief</u>. When you believe, then God ***(Php.2:13) ... worketh in you both to will and to work, for his good pleasure.***

 (Heb.3:19) And we see that they were not able to <u>enter in</u> ("Enter in" to what? They were unable to enter in to the "rest," which is ceasing from your own struggling and striving to be your own savior.) ***because of <u>unbelief</u>.*** Or, as we've seen, "because of disobedience." ***(Heb.4:1) <u>Let us fear</u> therefore*** (This is about to tell us something that we <u>should</u> fear.)**, lest haply, <u>a promise being left of entering into his rest</u>, any one of you should seem to have come short of it.** Remember God's promises. Don't waste your time with the world. There's only a little time left for you to draw near to the Lord, for you to put the Word of God in your heart, and for you to be bold in the faith. Start exercising your faith for things now. Start trusting God for things now. He's given promises that cover every one of your needs. Worry less and less about taking care of yourself, and worry more and more about walking by faith in Him. If you want to fear anything, fear that you're leaving out even one of God's promises. They are your truth. They are the shelter of His wings. They are your shield and buckler. They are what will protect you from the plagues that are coming upon this world.

(Heb.4:2) For indeed we have had good tidings preached unto us, even as also they: but the word of hearing did not profit them, because it was not united by faith with them that heard. (3) For we who have believed do enter into that rest; even as he hath said, As I sware in my wrath, They shall not enter into my rest: although the works were finished from the foundation of the world. The works are finished. We just enter into the works of God, the works that He has already completed from the foundation of the world. From the beginning, what He spoke would come to pass <u>is</u> coming to pass. Is what He spoke coming to pass with <u>you</u>? God's Word will prevail. His Word is our shield and buckler. It is our truth. It is our protection, but we need to mix faith with that Word, so that we will be the righteous vessels through whom God will overcome this world. Oh, praise the Lord! Praise the Lord!

(Psa.91:5) Thou shalt not be afraid for the terror by night, Nor for the <u>arrow</u> that flieth by day. There are both spiritual and literal "arrows" that the Lord speaks about, and I'd like first to take a look at a spiritual arrow that He says we should not fear. ***(Psa.64:1) Hear my voice, O God, in my complaint: Preserve my life from <u>fear of the enemy</u>.*** We've seen that if you fear the enemy, then you don't believe what God says in Psalm 91, but here the psalmist, who is David, is asking for help to conquer this fear. ***(2) Hide me from the secret counsel of <u>evil-doers</u>*** (There are evil-doers everywhere and they're coming out of the Church, right and left. Praise God for that, because He is bringing a separation.)***, From the <u>tumult</u>*** (In other words, "Hide me from the confusion, turmoil, and trouble.") ***of the workers of iniquity: (3) Who have whet their tongue like a sword, And have aimed their <u>arrows</u>, <u>even bitter words</u>.*** He tells us not to fear the "arrow that flieth by day." In this case, the "arrow" is "bitter words," and of course, we know that people are going to speak against the righteous, but we are not to fear what they can do to us.

(Psa.64:3) Who have whet their tongue like a sword, And have aimed their arrows, even bitter words, (4) That they may shoot in secret places at the perfect: Suddenly do they shoot at him, and fear not. (5) They encourage themselves in an evil purpose (Many times your enemies will gather together against you.)***; They commune of laying snares privily...*** So they're trying to trap you. The Pharisees came together to try to trap Jesus in His words (Matthew 22:15; Mark 12:13; Luke 11:54; etc.), but He knew, by the Holy Spirit, exactly what they were doing, and the Holy Spir-

Believe the Truth and Be Set Free

it gave Him wisdom to answer. *(5) They encourage themselves in an evil purpose; They commune of laying snares privily; They say, Who will see them? (6) They search out iniquities; We have accomplished, [say they,] a diligent search: And the inward thought and the heart of every one is deep. (7)* <u>*But God will shoot at them;*</u> <u>*With an arrow suddenly shall they be wounded*</u>*. (8) So they shall be made to stumble, their own tongue being against them...* Whatever they say, they're going to reap, because that's what they're sowing (Galatians 6:7).

Of course, you don't want to fight fire with fire. You don't want to "wrestle with flesh and blood," for what you sow, you also will reap. God tells us how to fight with these people, and it's not in the flesh (2 Corinthians 10:3-5; Ephesians 6:10-17). *(Psa.64:8) So they shall be made to stumble, their own tongue being against them: All that see them shall wag the head. (9) And all men shall fear; And they shall declare the work of God, And shall wisely consider of his doing. (10) The righteous shall be glad in the Lord, and shall take refuge in him; And all the upright in heart shall glory.* You see, if we serve the Lord and not our flesh, and therefore don't retaliate the way the world does, the Lord will defend us. He will use us as an example and people will be brought into the Kingdom. That's what He's saying here.

A little different kind of "arrow" is where God speaks of Babylon conquering the nations and then, afterward at the end, being conquered by the nations. *(Jer.25:29) For lo, I begin to work evil at the city which is called by my name; and should <u>ye</u>* (This is speaking of Babylon, "the great eagle.") *be utterly unpunished? (30) There-*

fore prophesy thou against them all these words, and say unto them, the Lord will roar from on high, and utter his voice from his holy habitation; <u>he will mightily roar against his fold</u>... These are the people who are left, the ones that are still not protected at the end of the Tribulation, because in type, Babylon fell at the end of 70 years, which in our day is 7 years. These are the people that are still not walking in the Lord and are still not abiding in the Ark at the end. These are the people that have been separated; they are the tares. They consider themselves Christians, but they're not. What is going to happen to them? **(Heb.6:7) *For the land which hath drunk the rain that cometh oft upon it, and bringeth forth herbs meet for them for whose sake it is also tilled, receiveth blessing from God: (8) but if it beareth thorns and thistles, it is rejected and nigh unto a curse; <u>whose end is to be burned</u>.***

(Jer.25:30) *Therefore prophesy thou against them all these words, and say unto them, the Lord will roar from on high, and utter his voice from his holy habitation; he will mightily roar against his fold; he will give a shout, as they that tread <u>[the grapes]</u>...* He's talking about the "grapes of wrath." **(Rev.14:19) *And the angel cast his sickle into the earth, and gathered the vintage of the earth, and cast it into the winepress, the [great winepress,] of the wrath of God. (20) And the winepress are trodden without the city, and there came out blood from the winepress, even unto the bridles of the horses, as far as a thousand and six hundred furlongs.*** These are the people who are going into the "great and terrible day of the Lord" (Joel 1:15, 2:31; Malachi 4:5; Acts 2:20; 1 Thessalonians 5:2; etc.), the day of God's wrath. They were not found to have borne the fruit of Jesus Christ, so they did not go up in the Ark.

(Jer.25:30) Therefore prophesy thou against them all these words, and say unto them, the Lord will roar from on high, and utter his voice from his holy habitation; he will mightily roar against his fold; he will give a shout, as they that tread [the grapes], against all the inhabitants of the earth. (31) A <u>noise</u> shall come even to the end of the earth; for the Lord hath a controversy with the nations; he will enter into judgment with all flesh... I believe this "noise" is that last nuclear war, as if arrows are flying from nation to nation, but He tells us not to fear those arrows, either. We know from Noah's testimony that they were warned by God in advance, ***(Gen.7:4) For yet <u>seven days</u>***, (In type, that's the seven years of the Tribulation in our time.), ***and I will cause it to rain upon the earth forty days and forty nights; and every living thing that I have made will I destroy from off the face of the ground.*** Then, for the 40 days while the Flood was coming upon the earth, Noah was in the Ark. He was in safety as he was beholding "the reward of the wicked," and it didn't touch him. ***(Gen.7:17) And the flood was <u>forty days</u> upon the earth; and the waters increased, and bare up the ark, <u>and it was lifted up above the earth</u>.*** Psalm 91 is also going to be manifested as a "Psalm 91 Passover" for the saints during the last 40 days before the Ark lifts off. This is that time right here, from the time that America is attacked by Russia and China until the end of that 40 days, when God's people are going to be preserved in the Ark before the Ark lifts off in a repetition of history. We know that the timing is exactly the same as at the end of the book of Daniel (Daniel 12:11-13). It's confirmed there, so we know that that's how God is going to preserve His people. [Editor's Note: For a more complete discussion of the Tribulation, see *Hidden Manna for the End Times,* which is available without charge at ubm1.org page=ubmbooks as a PDF.]

(Jer.25:31) A noise shall come even to the end of the earth; for the Lord hath a controversy with the nations; he will enter into judgment with all flesh: as for the wicked, he will give them to the sword, saith the Lord. (32) Thus saith the Lord of hosts, Behold, <u>evil shall go forth from nation to nation</u> (This is talking about those "arrows."), ***and a <u>great tempest</u> shall be raised up from the uttermost parts of the earth.*** Nuclear storms are going to be raised up. ***(33) And the slain of the Lord shall be at that day from one end of the earth even unto the other end of the earth*** (This is truly the "flood."): ***they shall not be lamented, neither gathered, nor buried; they shall be dung upon the face of the ground. (34) Wail, ye shepherds,..."*** (So there are shepherds left here, with their folds.), ***and cry; and wallow [in ashes,] ye <u>principal of the flock</u>*** (These are the "great men" of "Christianity."); ***for the days of your slaughter and of your dispersions are fully come, and ye shall fall like a goodly vessel.*** They fall in the flood of the Great and Terrible Day of the Lord. ***(35) And the shepherds shall have no way to flee, nor the principal of the flock to escape. (36) A voice of the cry of the shepherds, and the wailing of the principal of the flock! for the Lord layeth waste***

their pasture. (37) And the peaceable folds are brought to silence because of the fierce anger of the Lord. (38) He hath left his covert, as the lion; for their land is become an astonishment because of the fierceness of the oppressing [sword,] and because of his fierce anger. His fierce anger is against the apostates who have refused His grace and have refused His Word. They have refused His truth, which would have protected and preserved them and would have had them in the Ark, abiding in the Ark of Jesus Christ. But they have refused His grace, His Word, His truth, and have persecuted His saints.

(Psa.91:6) For the pestilence that walketh in darkness (No doubt, both nuclear and biological weapons will be released at that time, all over the world. There will be pestilence everywhere.)*, Nor for the destruction that wasteth at noonday.* The Lord is saying here, "Thou shalt not be afraid for these things." God's people will not be afraid. Great preservation is coming for God's people. *(8) Only with thine eyes shalt thou behold, And see the reward of the wicked.* God's people are going to be preserved from all of this. We have His promise. *(7) A thousand shall fall at thy side, And ten thousand at thy right hand; [But] it shall not come nigh thee.* Praise God! That's God's Word. If you confess it and believe it, God will do it!

CHAPTER FIVE

How to War Against Fear

Father, in the Name of Jesus, we thank You for being our Lord and our Savior. Thank You that, as Jeremiah chapter 3 says, we can call You, "my Father." Lord, we thank You so much for that relationship. We thank You so much for Your kindness. We thank You so much that we don't live under the Old Covenant. Thank You for grace, Lord. Thank You for mercy. Thank You for the outpouring of Your Spirit to empower us to be what we could never be otherwise. Thank You that now it's not us, but Christ in us, Who does the work. Lord, You've asked us just to repent and believe, and we thank You that You even grant us the grace to repent and the faith to believe. Thank You for grace, Lord. Thank You so much, Lord, for doing this work in us. Thank You for getting us ready for the plagues that are about to come upon this world, Lord, just like in the days of Egypt when You preserved Your people in Goshen. Thank You, Lord, for Your grace to rise up in us, to bring to our remembrance everything that You have said to us to defend us against these judgments coming upon the world. Thank You for our Passover Lamb, Jesus Christ. Thank You and help us to eat all of the Lamb so that we have a Passover of the judgments of the curse of this world. Hallelujah! Amen!

God is preparing us to be immune to the judgments of this world by filling us with His promises and renewing our minds with His Word. ***(Rom.12:2) And be not fashioned according to this world: but be ye transformed by the renewing of your mind, that ye may prove what is the good and acceptable and***

perfect will of God. Praise be to God! Well, we've been looking at Psalm 91 because there's a pretty good "vaccination" there, and I'd like to back-up a few verses. ***(Psa.91:5) Thou shalt not be afraid for the <u>terror by night</u>, Nor for the arrow that flieth by day; (6) For the <u>pestilence that walketh in darkness</u>*** (Some things you can't see, but you know they are dangerous. You may see the signs of them around you, and, of course, the devil takes full advantage of that by coming against your mind.)***, Nor for the destruction that wasteth at noonday.*** So we are not to fear the dangers that we can see. Some of our biggest problems are the things that we see, but, of course, we also worry about the things we can't see. If you <u>see</u> somebody around you start sneezing or coughing, the first thing the devil throws at you is, "Uh oh! Now you're going to catch it, too!" Folks, what people die of is fear of the <u>curse</u>, from which Jesus has <u>delivered</u> us (Exodus 12; Galatians 3:13). We have a Passover Lamb that we've eaten. ***(1Co.5:7) Purge out the old leaven, that ye may be a new lump, even as ye are unleavened. For our passover also hath been sacrificed, [even] Christ.*** Our Lamb, Jesus Christ, has already been sacrificed. The Bible says, ***(Psa.103:2) Bless the Lord, O my soul, And forget not all his benefits: (3) Who forgiveth <u>all</u> thine iniquities; <u>Who healeth all</u> thy diseases.*** We don't die of diseases, of plagues, of curses; no, we die of <u>unbelief</u> and <u>fear</u>.

The devil takes us out, many times, with the warfare against our mind and we lose our faith. Then we die because of fear, which is faith in the curse. We need to be ***(2Co.10:5) casting down imaginations, and every high thing that is exalted against the knowledge*** *of God, and bringing every thought into captivity to the obedience of Christ.* Jesus told us, *(Luk.21:25) And there shall be signs in the sun and moon and stars; and upon the earth distress of nations, in perplexity for the roaring of the sea and the billows.* You can see the "roaring of the sea and the billows" as being the anger of the nations against one another, because the Bible tells us that the "waters" represent peoples, nations, and tongues (Revelation 17:15). Obviously, the things that nations are exporting around the world, such as terrorism and anarchy and so on, are making a lot of people fearful. *(Luk.21:26)* <u>*Men fainting for fear, and for expectation of the things which are coming on the world*</u>*: for the powers of the heavens shall be shaken.* The *King James* translation says, "Men's hearts failing them for fear," but the numeric pattern and the Greek both show that "fainting" is a much better interpretation. "Men fainting for fear, and for <u>expectation</u>..." What is this "expectation"? It's believing in the curse. It's believing these things are all a threat to you, and seeing in your imagination all the terrible things that could happen to you because of them. That's why we're told to cast down imaginations. The devil prepares us to fail through our imaginations. Again, people aren't dying because of the curse. The Lord took care of that. They're dying because of unbelief and fear, which looses the curse. Faith in the promises binds the curse.

In every instance where you're put into a position of being threatened, remember that the devil and his army, his angels, see in both the spirit realm and in the physical realm. They coordinate their attacks on you to coincide with the things that you see with your eyes or the things you hear with your ears or, especially, the imaginations in your mind about the things that could happen. They will pounce on you so that you are struck, suddenly, with this temptation to fear. You know, we think in pictures and the devil will take you over with those pictures. He will put fear in you exactly as this verse is talking about here. You need to stop immediately and make war on him when he attacks you with these things or he will just take you away, and then you will be at the mercy of the judgments that are around you. We've seen from the Scriptures, very plainly, that Jesus bore the whole curse upon Himself when He was upon the Cross (Galatians 3:13). We've also seen, **(Rom.10:10) For with the heart man believeth unto righteousness; <u>and with the mouth confession is made unto salvation</u>.** You need to confess Psalm 91 in the midst of the trouble, not while you're in church. In the midst of the trouble, when there's an opportunity for you to give the devil authority to take you away, the Gospel is the power of God to save the one who believes it (Romans 1:16). In the midst of the trouble, you make your confession because faith without works is dead (James 2:17). Whenever your actions are totally contrary to faith, the devil takes that as his authority. Jesus told us, **(Mat.18:18) Verily I say unto you, what things soever ye shall bind on earth shall be bound in heaven; and what things soever ye shall loose on earth shall be loosed in heaven.**

So the devil is going to make war on the saints with the judgments that are coming upon the world. And most people don't know that those judgments are coming upon the world not to hurt the saints, but to deliver the saints, because these judgments are going to separate the wheat from the tares. I want to share with you a revelation from

Dimitru Duduman that fits exactly what we're talking about here. This vision was given to Dimitru in May of 1993 when he was living in Oregon. It describes our rights in Christ and how the Blood is applied through casting down fear and doubt and speaking the promise, which is, of course, our Sword of the Spirit. He said, *It was getting dark. Then, suddenly, it turned pitch black.* It's interesting that we can look around us right now and see that it's starting to get dark. People are mentioning to me that they're seeing many things that they've never seen before. They're seeing Christians, lukewarm Christians, turn toward darkness, and governments that have been taken over by the beast. *It was as if the whole world had gone dark at that moment.* I think we're on the verge of that darkness coming, folks. It will be great tribulation and we need to be ready for it. We need to not waste our time. We need to have our armor on. *All the people were in a frenzy. They became disoriented, and some were even screaming.* That sounds exactly like the verse we just read in Luke 21. *After some time, we heard the sound of an army approaching.* This is talking about the devil's army, multitudes of demon spirits that make war on the saints and also inhabit men, who physically make war on the saints. We call that the "beast."

Soon, we saw them coming out of the black mist. All were dressed in black, except for one. That one seemed to be their leader. He was dressed in a red robe with a thick, black belt over his waist. On his head, he had a sign. As I looked, I saw that in his hand, he held the same kind of sharp spear as everyone else in his army. "I am Lucifer," he exclaimed. "I am the king of this world. I've come to make war against the Christians." This war is about to start, folks. The darkness is covering the earth, and this war is about to start. *It looked as though all the Christians were huddled together in one big group. Some began to cry when they heard this. Others began to tremble, while some just stood, without saying anything.* What is this that's already happening to God's people in this revelation? It's Satan's warfare against them. They're crying, they're trembling, they're fearful because of the threat they can <u>see</u>. What is the devil's army? It's those spirits that attack your mind, spirits such as fear and doubt and grief and condemnation and lust and hatred and unforgiveness and rejection and addictions of different kinds and occultic things and thefts and lying and on and on… Everybody has trials with these spirits making war against them as the spirits seek to bring them into their realm. Praise the Lord that we've been delivered of this by Jesus Christ! All the promises that are given to us in the Word of God are what we can use as our Sword to set each other free.

Well, when they saw Satan's army coming in great force, many people trembled and were fearful, but some didn't do anything because they weren't moved by what they <u>saw</u>. *Lucifer continued to speak. "All of those that want to fight against my army, and think they can be victorious, go to the right…"* Obviously, that's where the sheep go; they go to the right. If you're not convinced that you can be victorious against Satan's army, it's because you don't have enough of the Word of God in your mind to really do warfare with him. We have to have on that "helmet of salvation" (Ephesians 6:17). We have to have the knowledge of the <u>fact</u> that we are protected, we are delivered, it is finished, Jesus has overcome the world, and the only thing left is for us to enter into those works that were finished from the foundation of the world (Hebrews chapters 3 and 4). How do we do that? We enter into those works by <u>faith</u>. Everything that Jesus did, the body of Christ is going to do (John 14:12). He had victory, He knew he could conquer Satan. Satan trembled before Him, because Jesus knew Who He was. He was a Son of God. He is the only begotten Son of God, in Whom we, too, are sons. Jesus said, **(Joh.20:21) ... Peace be unto you: as the Father hath sent me, even so send I <u>you</u>.** If you know who you are, and you know what God says about you, the devil trembles before you, but he can convince a lot of people who justify themselves and are not really believers of the Word of God.

So the devil said, *"All of those that want to fight against my army, and think they can be victorious, go to the right, and those that fear me, go to the left."* Why does God permit this war? He is permitting this war to separate the sheep from the goats. In these end times, the Lord says that He is going to spew the lukewarm out of his mouth (Revelation 3:16). He's not going to have any fence riders; you're going to be in either one camp or the other. This warfare of the devil against the Church is going to bring the separation, and notice what he says next. *Only about a quarter of the group stepped to the right.* That means three-quarters of what were called "Christians" in this revelation were no threat to the devil, and he was going to conquer them. *All the others went to the left.* That was three-quarters of them who went to the left because of fear. Those of them who thought they would be victorious over Satan were only a quarter of the Christians, and I don't think that is really a stretch at all. Even today, there are very few people that are actually chasing Satan, and the rest are all being chased by him, which is exactly what the Bible tells us. **(Luk.11:21) When the strong [man] fully armed guardeth his**

own court, his goods are in peace: (22) but when a stronger than he shall come upon him, and overcome him, he taketh from him his whole armor wherein he trusted, and divideth his spoils. (23) He that is not with me is against me; and he that gathereth not with me scattereth.

Then, Lucifer ordered his army, "Destroy those on the right." The army began to advance and quickly surround the Christians on the right. Remember that's the smaller group, the one-quarter. *And as they began to close in on us, a powerful light appeared, and encircled us. Then, the angel of the Lord spoke, "Take out your Swords and fight! Defend yourselves! Be victorious over the enemy." "What swords?" a man in the group asked. "The Word of the Lord is your Sword," the angel answered.* Yes, take out your Sword and <u>fight</u> and be victorious over the enemy. The devil can do nothing against it; there is no weapon that he can use to defend against your Sword, which is the Word of God. It is the true Word of God. It cannot be denied. It will fulfill the purpose that God sent it for (Luke 1:37), but we have to <u>use</u> it. You can give-in to the temptations of fear and doubt that the devil fires at you in the midst of the fiery trial, or you can fight. Be sure to confess your sins (1 John 3:21) so that the devil can't use condemnation against you, because then you can swing your Sword with bold faith and you will win. **(2Ti.1:7) For God gave us not a spirit of fearfulness; but of power and love and <u>discipline</u>.** The word translated as "discipline" comes from the Greek *sóphrón* meaning "of sound mind; self-controlled; balanced." Any fear that comes against you is from the devil; it's not from God. Jesus told us that we should fear only God (Matthew 10:28). The fear of the <u>Lord</u> is good, because every child should fear that their father will spank them if they're going in the wrong direction. In that way, we should always fear God, but the Lord isn't going to lead you by fear all the time, and if you feel that way, you're probably being moved by the devil. Scripture tells us, ***(Rom.8:15) <u>For ye received not the spirit of bondage again unto fear</u>; but ye received the spirit of adoption, whereby we cry, Abba, Father.***

Since God's method of leading His children is not fear, whenever fear comes upon you, you need to make war against it immediately. You need to stop whatever you're doing and cast down the thoughts that the devil is putting in your mind. Cast down those pictures that the devil is putting in your mind, and make war against that spirit, because otherwise he will conquer you. You may have all the knowledge that you need but you won't be able to even hear it in the midst of this emotion of fear that has come upon you. So stop and make war. The devil can't stand before you if you use your Sword. You don't necessarily have to quote the Word of God to conquer the devil, but you do have to agree with the Word of God to conquer the devil. You have to know what the Word of God says in order to speak in agreement with the Word of God, so if you're not sure about what the Scriptures say, you need to spend more time in the Word.

Let me go on with Dumitru Duduman's revelation here. *When we understood what the angel meant, we began to quote verses from the Bible. Then, suddenly, as if we were one voice, we began to sing a song.* That's the thing about songs; they bring people into one accord, and there's power in agreement. Jesus promised us, ***(Mat.18:19) Again I say unto you, that if two of you shall agree on*** *earth as touching anything that they shall ask, it shall be done for them of my Father who is in heaven. (20) For where two or three are gathered together in my name, there am I in the midst of them.* What happens when there are more than two or three of you in agreement? *(Deu.32:30) How should one chase a thousand, And two put ten thousand to flight, Except their Rock had sold them, And the Lord had delivered them up?* Wow! One will chase a thousand and two will chase ten thousand; that's <u>multiplied</u> power, so it's a blessing for us to be in agreement with each other and with the Word of God. That's why God has given us His Word. Of course, it does no good if you're in agreement with a lot of apostates because no matter how large a group they might be, you still will have no power. The devil is going to show us this in Dumitru's revelation. He's going to conquer these people. The devil wants to make war, and he wants to take out the people who are a threat to him. He'd like to take out their physical life and he'd like to take out their spiritual life, because they're doing him damage. He will make war on you but he's not able to do anything that God doesn't permit him to do. You see, God permits the devil to come try us in order to build our faith. Faith is like a muscle. If your faith isn't tried, it's not going to get stronger. We go through things to try our faith, and in the process, we also learn how to quickly pull out our Sword and use it to conquer the enemy.

So the smaller group began to quote verses from the Bible and they began to sing a song. *Our voices thundered so loudly that the dark army began to retreat.* These are the people on the right. These are the sheep. *They did not have the courage to come against us anymore. Lucifer, filled with rage, turned to those on the left.* Those on the left are the three-quarters majority of the Christians. *"You, who all of your life have been trying to please two masters, because you could not stand against me, I have the power to destroy you."* That is true. He's been given that power to destroy people who are in unbelief and, in these end times, we have very little time left to learn to walk in the Kingdom of God. Satan's going to be cast down. He knows he has a short time left (Revelation 12:9,12). He's going to fight furiously, he and his army and the people whom they inhabit are going to come against us with great fury, but we have a weapon that they can't resist. The problem is that far too many of God's people don't use that weapon; they don't use the promises of the Word of God. The Word is our Sword and the demons cannot stand up to that. We see here that those people who, all their life, tried to serve two masters, had no protection. They tried to serve both self and the Lord; they were double-minded (James 1:7-8). They were found to be lukewarm and there was no protection for these people (Revelation 3:16).

Saints, I'll just let you know right now that you need to get your armor on, you need to be on fire for God, and you need to learn to fight. **(Eph.6:10) Finally, be strong in the Lord, and in the strength of his might. (11) Put on the whole armor of God, that ye may be able to stand against the wiles of the devil. (12) For our wrestling is not against flesh and blood, but against the principalities, against the powers, against the world-rulers of this darkness, against the spiritual [hosts] of wickedness in the heavenly [places]. (13) Wherefore take up the whole armor of God, that ye may be able to withstand in** *the evil day, and, having done all, to stand. (14) Stand therefore, having girded your loins with truth, and having put on the breastplate of righteousness, (15) and having shod your feet with the preparation of the gospel of peace; (16) withal taking up the shield of faith, wherewith ye shall be able to quench all the fiery darts of the evil [one]. (17) And take the helmet of salvation, and the sword of the Spirit, which is the word of God.*

In this revelation, when Lucifer said, "I have the power to destroy you," who gave him that power? <u>They</u> did. They are the ones who have authority on earth to bind or to loose, and here they have loosed Satan because of their unbelief, their double-mindedness, and their lukewarmness. *He then ordered his army to attack. It was a total massacre. The ones on the left could not defend themselves.* Could you imagine that three-quarters of Christianity could not defend themselves right now? I can. It seems fairly obvious. *One by one, they all fell. This killing seemed to go on for a long time* (I believe that this killing is not just physical, but spiritual, because many of these people are going to lose their eternal life.), *and after a while, we could actually smell the stench of the dead.* "Why could they not be protected also?" someone asked. The angel answered, "Because all their lives, they have been lukewarm. Because of their hypocrisy, the true church has been blasphemed." That's speaking, of course, of the quarter who went to the right, the sheep. They had been blasphemed. They had been accused by the world because of the hypocrisy of the false church, the three-quarters of the people who went to the left. *"They have brought disrespect to the Word of God."* It's true; today we see people just scoff at the Word of God.

Even Christians scoff at the Word of God. In the midst of a trial, you may share the Word of God with them but they'll choose to cling to the idol, the stronghold in their mind. They'll choose their idol instead of *(2Co.10:5) casting down imaginations, and every high thing that is exalted against the knowledge of God, and bringing every thought into captivity to the obedience of Christ.*

Satan has been able to set-up a stronghold in their mind because they're worshiping false gods. They have a false Jesus, as Paul said. *(2Co.11:4) For if he that cometh preacheth <u>another Jesus</u>, whom we did not preach, or if ye receive a <u>different spirit</u>, which ye did not receive, or a <u>different gospel</u>, which ye did not accept, ye do well to bear with [him].* That false Jesus can't save you because he's not the Word of God. The true Jesus is the Word of God; the true Jesus is our Sword. He can save. He will save all those who respect Him. All through the Old Testament, God warns us about the danger of worshiping idols, and it's sad that so many Christians today worship a Jesus that does not exist. Their "Jesus" is nothing more than demons (Leviticus 17:7; Deuteronomy 32:17; 1 Corinthians 10:20) that they have set up as their idols and they will not save. Satan does not cast out Satan, as Jesus told the Pharisees. *(Mat.12:26) … Every kingdom divided against itself is brought to desolation; and every city or house divided against itself shall not stand: (26) and if Satan casteth out Satan, he is divided against himself; how then shall his kingdom stand?* If you are following, worshiping, and putting your faith in a false Jesus, he will not save you. "Anti-Christ" means not only "against Christ," but also "in the place of Christ." The devil likes to replace the real Jesus with a false Jesus because that way, when you put your trust in him, he will fail you. And this is what's going to happen in the days to come, according to Dimitru's dream. Three-quarters of the church is going to have their "Jesus" fail them. God does not answer when you trust in your false Jesus because then you would be giving credit to your false Jesus, and other people would trust in this false Jesus, too.

When that happens, when their false Jesus fails to save them, people accuse God. They complain, "But I believed!" No, they didn't believe because their faith was in a false Jesus who couldn't save. Satan will never cast out Satan. The angel went on to say of those who were killed by Lucifer's army, *"They were not clean."* You have no authority to swing the Sword unless you're "clean," unless your conscience is not condemning you. **(1Jn.3:21) Beloved, <u>if our heart condemn us not</u>, we have boldness toward God; (22) and whatsoever we ask we receive of him, because we keep his commandments and do the things that are pleasing in his sight.** The devil conquers those people who are walking in sin and rebellion and defilement. Even though they intellectually know all about faith and how it works, they're not able to <u>use</u> faith. It takes faith to <u>swing</u> the Sword. If you're unholy, the devil will pick that point of uncleanness to jump on you and condemn you so that you can't have faith. *As we continued to look, we saw the sun coming over the horizon.* I think that represents the coming of the Lord. *The black clouds began to break up, then they disappeared. Only one was left, the one on which Lucifer and his army stood. Lucifer looked at me, shaking his fist, and said, "I will destroy you, even if I have to throw my spear at you from here."* Then *that cloud disappeared. As I looked around, I began to see faces that I recognized from among our group. I saw a pastor from Bellflower, another from Indiana, one from Michigan, as well as many of my American friends. The first thought that came to my mind as I awoke was that this had been the last fight of the devil against the church. If we remain faithful, we will be victorious.* Yes! Amen.

So get ready, saints! Put on your armor, because this battle, the last war against the Church, is coming at us right now. **(Rev.13:1) ... And I saw a beast coming up out of the sea, having ten horns, and seven heads, and on his horns ten diadems, and upon his heads names of blasphemy. (7) And it was given unto him to make war with the saints, and to overcome them: and there was given to him authority over every tribe and people and tongue and nation.** The "beast" that's warring with the saints here is made up of all the fleshly vessels whom this army from the pit is going to inhabit. This awesome revelation from Dimitru Duduman shows us very clearly that if you don't walk holy before God, your faith is going to fail you. **(1Jn.3:19) Hereby shall we know that we are of the truth, and shall <u>assure our heart</u> before him** (You have to have this assurance in your heart if you're going to do battle with the devil. He knows everything about you.)**: (20) because if our heart condemn us, God is greater than our heart, and knoweth all things.** If you're condemned by what you know about yourself, just think what God knows about you (Psalm 139:1-24). However, if you're walking with the Lord by faith, it's only the things that you know about, but don't do, that He holds against you. It's not the things that you don't know. **(Jas.4:17) To him therefore that <u>knoweth</u>**

to do good, and doeth it not, to him it is sin.

Of course, if you're walking in rebellion against the Lord then your sins are not covered. ***(Heb.10:26) For <u>if we sin wilfully</u> after that we have received the knowledge of the truth, there remaineth no more a sacrifice for sins, (27) but a certain fearful expectation of judgment, and a fierceness of fire which shall devour the adversaries.*** In that case, you have no assurance in your heart, so the first time you get into trouble and you try to swing your Sword, the devil's going to jump on you like a mad dog. He's going to remind you of all of your sins and then you're not going to have any faith. ***(1Jn.3:21) Beloved, <u>if our heart condemn us not</u>, we have boldness toward God; (22) and whatsoever we ask we receive of him, because we keep his commandments and do the things that are pleasing in his sight.*** You know, we all have people who depend upon us: friends, relatives, people for whom we've prayed, children who are our responsibility. Scripture says, ***(Rom.14:7) For none of us liveth to himself, and none dieth to himself.*** The Lord wants to use us to save others and the day is coming when God is going to need you as a vessel of honor in the midst of many people. He is going to need you to save, to deliver, to bring the Gospel, and so on. Now, more than ever before in history, we need to repent and be sanctified. We need to walk holy before the Lord.

The Bible says, ***(Rom.6:11) Even so reckon ye also yourselves to be dead unto sin, but alive unto God in Christ Jesus.*** You see, the Lord has already delivered us by <u>faith</u>, and He uses our faith to <u>manifestly</u> deliver us. He uses the Word of God in our mouth, which is our confession, to manifestly deliver us from the power of sin. God is the One ***(Col.1:13) who delivered us out of the power of darkness, and translated us into the kingdom of the Son of his love.*** It happened at the Cross, and we need to confess it, but we won't be able to confess it in the midst of the fiery trial if we're walking in willful disobedience. We won't have any faith to swing our Swords. ***(Psa.91:7) A thousand shall fall at thy side, And ten thousand at thy right hand; [But] it shall not come nigh <u>thee</u>.*** He's talking about the person who is not afraid, the person who is in the secret place of the Most High because of their faith. He's talking about the person who is <u>confessing</u> that faith, the faith of Psalm 91. When He says, "A thousand shall fall at thy side, And ten thousand at thy right hand," do you suppose that some of those are Christians? Yes, I guarantee at least some of these people are what we call "Christians," and it's sad. The Lord cries when this happens, and we do, too.

    A multitude of people, obviously, are not prepared for what's about to come, but God can use your witness to them. You can share the true Gospel with many people who don't know the true, full Gospel. Other people have rejected the full Gospel and they are not prepared to swing their Sword at all. Remember that someone in the revelation had to ask, "What swords?" Before you go to battle, you ought to know <u>what</u> your Sword is, you ought to know <u>how</u> to swing it, and you ought to be <u>experienced</u> in using it, because ***(Rom.1:17) … the righteous shall live by <u>faith</u>.*** We don't have any choice, folks. The devil's not going to ask us if we want to make war with him; he's already making war with us. The people who are abiding in the secret place of the Most High, which is Jesus Christ, are ready to swing the Sword. They have repented of and confessed their sins, therefore they can be bold in their faith.

I've heard people say, usually from among the non-Spirit-filled groups, that Psalm 91 is for the Millennium or something silly like that, as if it's not true for us right now. Well, if you believe that, you have no Sword. You're going to be in the three-quarters group that goes to the left and is whipped by Satan in the end times. If you don't believe in the full Gospel and the power of the Spirit of God, how can you escape? If you don't believe in the gifts of the Holy Spirit and the promises of the Word of God, how can you escape? How can you escape "the pestilence that walketh in darkness" or "the destruction that wasteth at noonday"? Do you know enough of the Word of God to know that it's your <u>right</u> to escape these things? If you don't, you're not going to escape. Jesus said, **(Mat.9:29) ... According to your <u>faith</u> be it done unto you**, and **(Mat.8:13) ... As thou hast <u>believed</u>, [so] be it done unto thee.** Jesus <u>saw</u> the faith. **(Mat.9:2) And behold, they brought to him a man sick of the palsy, lying on a bed: and Jesus <u>seeing their faith</u> said unto the sick of the palsy, Son, be of good cheer; thy sins are forgiven. (3) And behold, certain of the scribes said within themselves, This man blasphemeth. (4) And Jesus knowing their thoughts said, Wherefore think ye evil in your hearts? (5) For which is easier, to say, Thy sins are forgiven; or to say, Arise, and walk? (6) But that ye may know that the Son of man hath authority on earth to forgive sins (then saith he to the sick of the palsy), Arise, and take up thy bed, and go up unto thy house. (7) And he arose, and departed to his house. (8) But when**

the multitudes saw it, they were afraid, and glorified God, who had given such <u>authority</u> unto men. He had the authority to administer the blessing when He saw the faith. The faith He saw was in <u>actions</u>, it wasn't just words, it wasn't just theology in somebody's head. He saw the actions, ***(Rom.10:10) for with the heart man believeth unto righteousness; and with the mouth confession is made unto salvation.***

Get prepared, saints. The war is coming. It's not going to wait on you. It's not going to wait on me. It's coming. It will be on time. If, as Joshua and Caleb, you don't believe the bad report but speak in agreement with the Word of God (Numbers 14:6-8), you will be like those people who did not worry about the giants. ***(Num.14:9) Only rebel not against the Lord, neither fear ye the <u>people of the land</u>*** (This is speaking of the giants in the Promised Land.)***; for they are bread for us: their defence is removed from over them, and the Lord is with us: <u>fear them not</u>.*** You'll be among those people who make it through the wilderness. You'll be among those people who enter into the Promised Land in your body. That's what they did. ***(Num.14:30) Surely ye shall not come into the land, concerning which I sware that I would make you dwell therein, save <u>Caleb the son of Jephunneh</u>, <u>and Joshua the son of Nun</u>.*** The rest did not; they died out there in that wilderness because of their murmuring, their complaining, and their unbelief (Numbers 14:28-32). They were constantly being tried by the devil. They constantly heard his horror stories in their head about what would happen to them because they couldn't see any water or other supply around them. The devil was constantly making war in their minds and he was beating them up badly. We're going to the same place. The Lord calls it the "wilderness" but it's also called the "Tribulation." That's where war is going to be made on the saints, and that's where a separation is going to be made. That's where a separation of the hot from the lukewarm and the cold, the sheep from the goats, and the wheat from the tares, is going to be made.

(Psa.91:7) A thousand shall fall at thy side, And ten thousand at thy right hand; [But] <u>it shall not</u> (Let me repeat that in case you missed what it says, ***<u>it shall not</u>***. And here it is again, just to be sure you read it correctly, ***<u>it shall not</u>***.) ***come nigh thee.*** Wow! What makes the difference between those who are taken out and those who remain? Well, it's something that we shouldn't leave out. ***(Heb.4:1) <u>Let us fear therefore</u>, lest haply, <u>a promise being left</u> of entering into his rest, any one of you should seem to have come short of it.*** The Lord is telling us to fear that we're not appropriating <u>all</u> the promises of God, <u>all</u> of the Word of God, because God created this to be our defense. ***(2) For indeed we have had good tidings preached unto us...*** Not just "good tidings" but awesome tidings! There are promises for any problem, and there are even promises that cover everything, such as ***(Mar.11:24) Therefore I say unto you, <u>All</u> things whatsoever ye pray and ask for, believe that ye received them, and ye shall have them.*** So if you can't remember one that fits your particular problem, Jesus gave us those "catch-all" promises you can use. ***(Heb.4:2) For indeed we have had <u>good tidings</u>*** (That's the Gospel, the Good News.) ***preached unto us, even as also they: but the word of hearing did not profit them, because it was not united by <u>faith</u>***

with them that heard. It does you no good to go to Sunday school; it does you no good to read your Bible unless you're going to exercise faith in what you're reading, and it doesn't matter if your church is in agreement or not. Don't leave out one promise as your promise; take each promise as if it's been made personally to you because any promise you leave out is a Sword you're not using. That's "sitting" on your Sword.

(Heb.4:3) For we who have believed do enter into that rest; even as he hath said, As I sware in my wrath, They shall not enter into my rest: although <u>the works were finished from the foundation of the world</u>. The works of God have already been finished. Jesus was the Lamb slain from the foundation of the world (Revelation 13:8). As soon as God spoke it, it was so. He spoke the end from the beginning (Isaiah 46:10). He ordained a Savior before Adam ever fell. The whole plan was spoken into existence and nothing could stop it. It was so just because God said it, and everything that we see now that's coming to pass, is coming to pass because God said it. "The works were finished from the foundation of the world." Whose works do you want to enter into? You can enter into God's works through faith in His promises. You can be a vessel of honor. You can be a vessel who is in that one-quarter of Christians that conquers Satan, that knows they can conquer Satan. Or, you can be in the three-quarters of Christians that are lukewarm, that have their idolatrous religion but no Sword. They don't believe in the full Gospel, which you're going to need to make it through what's coming upon the earth. They don't believe in the in-filling of the Holy Spirit with the evidence of the gifts (Romans 11:29,12:6; 1 Corinthians 12:1-11,27-29; 1

Corinthians 14:1) so they're not empowered to walk where they need to go.

You know, when we enter into <u>His</u> rest, we enter into a rest from our enemies because they're dead; Jesus gave us total victory over them. Jesus said, **(Mat.28:18) ... <u>All authority hath been given unto me in heaven and on earth.</u>** That doesn't leave anything for the devil, folks. Then He turned to His disciples and He delegated that authority to them. **(Mat.18:18) Verily I say unto you, what things soever ye shall bind on earth shall be bound in heaven; and what things soever ye shall loose on earth shall be loosed in heaven. (19) Again I say unto you, that if two of you shall agree on earth as touching anything that they shall ask, it shall be done for them of my Father who is in heaven. (Joh.20:21) Jesus therefore said to them again, Peace be unto you: <u>as the Father hath sent me, even so send I you.</u>** Jesus had authority, and He spoke it, and the devils trembled. That <u>same</u> Jesus lives in you. To the extent that you humble yourself to the Word of God, and you believe the Word, and you're becoming the Word made flesh, to that extent Jesus lives in you. All you have to do is cooperate with Him. **(Amo.3:3) Shall two walk together, except they have <u>agreed</u>?** If you want that same Jesus to live in you, to conquer your enemies, to speak out of you, to swing the Sword and to do the works, then <u>you</u> have to come into agreement with <u>Him</u>. When you read the Word of God, repent, change your mind and believe what it says. We have to agree with it so that we don't restrain it from coming out of us.

If you're uncomfortable confessing anything that's in the Word of God, if you're uncomfortable repeating it, this is how you know you've been taken captive by false religion and false doctrine. If some of the Word of God is not comfortable in your mouth, then naturally you're not going to let it flow out of you, but how "shall two walk together, except they have agreed?" God warned His people about bringing forth "strange children" that don't look like their Father (Hosea 5:7). The problem is with us, it's not with God. Being a Christian is being very unlike, very contrary, to the world. They're total opposites. If you want to please the world, you can't be a Christian. If you don't want to be sanctified from the ways of the world, you can't be a Christian. You can call yourself a "Christian," but you can't be one, because "Christian" means "Christ-like." We have to be willing to lose our life in order to gain our life (Luke 17:33). We have to be willing to be seen as different, even "peculiar." ***(1Pe.2:9KJV) But ye [are] a chosen generation, a royal priesthood, an holy nation, a peculiar people; that ye should shew forth the praises of him who hath called you out of darkness into his marvelous light.***

Jesus said there are just two men in the earth: Christ and anti-Christ (Matthew 24:40-41). There are only two corporate bodies in this earth. There's not going to be anyone left in the middle because God calls that being "lukewarm." ***(Rev.3:16) So because thou art lukewarm, and neither hot nor cold, I will spew thee out of my mouth.*** You have to make up your mind. Are you going to lose your life in order to gain your life? ***(2Co.4:16) Wherefore we faint not; but though our outward man is decaying, yet our inward man is renewed day by day.*** As you lose ground to the old man of self, you give ground to the spiritual man, ***(Col.1:27) ... Christ in***

you, the hope of glory. Jesus is not going to have any trouble with this warfare that's coming, and Jesus in you is not going to have any trouble, either, with this warfare that's coming, but how "Shall two walk together, except they have agreed?" We have to come into agreement with Him. We have to read the Word, and when we read the Word, we have to decide, "I don't care what some man says; I agree with what this says." Then it becomes comfortable for you to speak all of the Word of God, but there are so many people, so many who can't do that. They may read the Word of God, but instead of coming into agreement, they deliberately jump over anything that makes them uncomfortable. They've been taken captive and they need to repent.

When you read the Word of God, as the Lord told me many years ago, "Don't eat like a hog; eat like a cow." Cows are ruminants. That means a cow chews its food, then brings it back up and chews it again, brings it back up and chews it again. With a hog, it just goes right in one end and right out the other end. It doesn't even get digested. This Word has to be a part of us. We meditate on it. ***(Psa.1:2) But his delight is in the law of the Lord; And on his law doth he meditate day and night.*** We want to be disciples of Jesus. We want to learn to walk in His steps. When that Word just comes flowing out of you like a river of living water, look out devil! There isn't anything he can do against that. Jesus told His disciples, ***(Joh.14:12) Verily, verily, I say unto you, he that believeth on me, the works that I do shall he do also; and greater [works] than these shall he do; because I go unto the Father.*** And, ***(Joh.7:38) He that believeth on me, as the scripture hath said, from within him shall flow rivers of living water. (39) But this spa-***

ke he of the Spirit, which they that believed on him were to receive: for the Spirit was not yet [given]; because Jesus was not yet glorified. He also said, *(Joh.6:63) It is the spirit that giveth life; the flesh profiteth nothing: the words that I have spoken unto you are spirit, and are life.* When your words agree with His words, your words are His Spirit. The Lord recreates in us His Spirit by His Words, and we're able to recreate Jesus by speaking His words. We're supposed to sow the same seed that He sowed, that His disciples sowed, that His apostles sowed. We're supposed to sow the Word of God.

Never depart from the Word of God. God's people must learn that religion crumbles in the face of adversity. Religion is no defense against what's coming. Throughout history, the merely religious have crumbled before the advances of the devil. There is no defense but the Word of God. No helmet, no sword, no shield, but the Word of God. Use Psalm 91 like a Helmet, Sword, and Shield because it's a defense. It's called "The Soldier's Psalm" because so many of them have been saved by claiming it. You are a soldier for the Lord, so don't let anybody talk you out of Psalm 91. It's saved many lives and it's for today. It's a part of the blessings of God for the faithful.

The demons administer the curse of sin and death. *(Luk.10:17) And the seventy returned with joy, saying, Lord, <u>even the demons are subject unto us in thy name</u>.* (Wouldn't it be great if all Christians learned that lesson?) *(18) And he said unto them, I beheld Satan fallen as lightning from the heaven.* He was talking about exactly what they were doing. He and His disciples were casting him down. *(19) Behold, I*

have given you authority to tread upon serpents and scorpions, and over <u>all the power of the enemy</u>: and nothing shall in any wise hurt you. (20) Nevertheless in this rejoice not, that <u>the spirits are subject unto you</u>; but rejoice that your names are written in heaven. Some people think Jesus used "over all the power of the enemy" a little too loosely but no, He means exactly what He says, and we have to learn to exercise this authority. "Authority" is "the right to use God's power or restrain the devil's power." I'd rather have that kind of authority than personal fleshly power.

In fact, you can even have authority to use the devil's power. The apostle Paul did that several times (1 Corinthians 5:3-5; 1 Timothy 1:18-20). He turned people over to Satan for the destruction of the flesh so that the spirit would be saved in the day of the Lord. He used the devil's power, and the devil couldn't resist him. The devil had to do what Paul told him to do. It's the same today. Jesus said, "<u>All</u> authority hath been given unto me in heaven and on earth … Go <u>ye</u>, therefore…" He delegated that authority to His disciples to go and to use His power. You have the authority to use God's power. That's what the Word is all about. You can be transformed by the renewing of your mind (Romans 12:2), but someone whose mind is not renewed is not trustworthy. If they had power, they would do foolish things. However, when we repent and we accept the Word of God as our Word, our thought, our belief, that puts us in agreement with Jesus. When we're in agreement with Jesus, then we can walk together and Jesus can do works through us. ***(Mat.11:29) Take my <u>yoke</u>*** (That's the Greek word *zugos* derived from *zygós* and it's "something that unites or joins two elements to work together as one unit.") ***upon***

you, and learn of me; for I am meek and lowly in heart: and ye shall find rest unto your souls. "Take my yoke," Jesus said. Yoke yourself to Him. And so He says, ***(Luk.10:19) Behold, I have given you authority to tread upon serpents and scorpions, and over all the power of the enemy: and <u>nothing shall in any wise hurt you</u>.*** <u>Nothing</u> shall hurt you. Oh, praise God! Believe that! Meditate on that! Rejoice in that!

CHAPTER SIX

God's Wondrous Protection and Provision

Father, in the Name of Jesus, teach us, Lord, to walk by faith in You. Your Word says faith is more precious than gold, and we know that it will preserve us through the times to come, Lord. While the world is trusting in their gods, we'll trust in our God. We give thanks unto You, Lord. You can do anything but fail. You can't fail. We thank you so much, Father, for being with us and in us, for rising-up in us with Your strength and Your wisdom, Lord, to be what we need to be. Glory be to God! We love You! We appreciate You! We ask that You bring to our remembrance all things that You have spoken unto us, especially to raise-up a standard against the devil when he comes with his words and his floods of thoughts and temptations and so forth. We thank You so much, Lord, in Jesus' Name.

The Flood Analogy

Saints, we need to do "preventative maintenance." As the Lord taught me many years ago, just a little bit of preventative maintenance early on can save you an awful lot of trouble later. That means we study the Word of God and we boldly confess what the Lord has given unto us in His promises, because the protection that He gives us every day from the curses of this world, is just incredible. We've been going through the wonderful promises in Psalm 91, just enjoying God's Word, and we left off with, **(Psa.91:7) A thousand shall fall at thy side, And ten thousand at thy right hand; [But] it shall not**

come nigh thee. What an awesome promise! Of course, it's a promise to those who dwell in the secret place of the Most High, and we know that those who are dwelling in the secret place are abiding in Christ. He is "the secret place of the Most High" as in, ***(Psa.90:1) Lord, thou hast been our dwelling-place in all generations.*** And John said, ***(1Jn.2:24) As for you, let that abide in you which ye heard from the beginning.*** <u>***If that which ye heard from the beginning abide in you***</u>, <u>***ye also shall abide in the Son***</u>, <u>***and in the Father.***</u> Abiding in Christ is having that in you which you heard from the beginning. It doesn't matter that we've absorbed the teachings of our religion, we have to absorb the teachings of the Word of God. If we want His provision in the days to come, we have to remember the promises He's given us in the Word of God.

When we read, "A thousand shall fall at thy side, And ten thousand at thy right hand; [But] it shall not come nigh thee," we can see it's a perfect type of a Passover being fulfilled. I know this kind of protection is fulfilled in minor ways all the time, but that verse is a very good example. The Flood of Genesis is a good example of this, too, and we know it's also an example of the end-time "flood," which is not a literal, physical flood of water covering the earth, but a spiritual "flood" of judgments covering the earth. ***(Mat.24:37) And as [were] the days of Noah, so shall be the coming of the Son of man. (38) For as in those days which were before the flood they were eating and drinking, marrying and giving in marriage, until the day that Noah entered into the ark, (39) and they knew not until the flood came, and took them all away*** (Of course, Jesus is not talking about the rapture here. He's talking about the Flood taking away the wicked. He says, "they knew not"; the righteous always know, but they "knew not."***); so shall be the coming of the Son of man. (40) Then shall two men be in the field; one is <u>taken</u>, and one is left: (41) two women [shall be] grinding at the mill; one is <u>taken</u>, and one is left.*** Now this "taken" is not talking about taking the wicked away, as so many preachers claim. "Taken" here is the Greek word, *paralambanó*, and it means "called to one's side in an affectionate manner," as in, "to take one's betrothed to his home." This is God, calling His saints aside, and these two verses are the only place *paralambanó* is used in the New Testament in this form. It's very clear that God wanted us to know that He was going to take His people out of this terrible flood.

I know that many people think the "flood" in verse 38 is talking about the Tribulation, but it's not. As a matter of fact, as we see from the text, God is saying that the "flood" there is a type of an end-time flood, so we can look for a type and a shadow in the Flood of Genesis. There, God told Noah, ***(Gen.7:4) <u>For yet seven days</u>, and I will cause it to rain upon the earth forty days and forty nights*** (So <u>after</u> seven days, there was going to come a flood for forty days and forty nights.)***; and every living thing that I have made will I destroy from off the face of the ground.*** In that part, He's made us the promise of the covenant of the rainbow, the promise that He's not ever again going to destroy every living thing (Genesis 9:11-17). This is very plain: <u>after</u> seven days of Daniel's seventieth week (Daniel 9:24-27), which we call the Tribulation, the "flood" is coming. First the Tribulation of seven days, then the 40 days begins the flood. In type, Noah's seven "days" are seven years. In type, Daniel's seventieth week is a *shabua*, meaning a "seven," a period of seven years. After those seven years, seen from the timing in Noah and Daniel, comes another year.

If we back up a few chapters, we find, ***(Gen.7:11) In the six hundredth year of Noah's life, in the second month, on the seventeenth day of the month, on the same day were all the fountains of the great deep broken up, and the windows of heaven were opened. ... (Gen.8:14) And in the second month, on the seven and twentieth day of the month, was the earth dry. (15) And God spake unto Noah, saying, (16) Go forth from the ark...*** So he went forth from the ark on the 365th day. In those days, according to the theologians, the earth had a 354-day year, and as we can see from these two different timings, 365 comes to ten days over a year. The timing goes from 354 days to 364 days, and Noah left the ark in what we would call a solar year. So we have a year here, a year after the "For yet seven days," and we've seen that those seven days represent seven years. After those seven years comes a year called the "great and terrible day of the Lord" (Joel 2:31; Malachi 4:5; etc.), or the "day of God's wrath" (Job 20:28; Zephaniah 1:15,2:2; Romans 2:5; etc.) These are synonymous terms all through the Bible and according to Matthew 24, a type and a shadow of the end times.

(Gen.7:17) And the flood was <u>forty days</u> upon the earth; and the waters increased, and bare up the ark, and it was lifted up above the earth. We see that the ark stood on the earth for 40 days <u>before</u> it was lifted up, and that's 40 days into what we call the "great and terrible day of the Lord," or the "day of God's wrath," or the "day of God's vengeance" (Isaiah 61:2). This is very important to understand. As a matter of fact, this year is spoken of in other places, such as in Isaiah 34, where the whole chapter speaks of this "day of God's wrath." ***(Isa.34:8) For the Lord hath a day of vengeance, a year of recompense for the cause of Zion.*** This is "payback" time. This year is all about recompense to the wicked who have tormented and persecuted God's people.

I'll go back to the beginning for just a little bit but I'm not going to spend much time here on this. ***(Isa.34:2) For the Lord hath indignation against all the nations, and wrath against all their host: he hath utterly destroyed them, <u>he hath delivered them to the slaughter</u>.*** That's what this year is. It's a year of slaughter. It's a year of the flood destroying the wicked of the earth. ***(3) Their slain also shall be cast out, and the stench of their dead bodies shall come up; and the mountains shall be melted with their blood. (4) And all the host of heaven shall be dissolved, <u>and the heavens shall be rolled together as a scroll</u*** (As you know, this doesn't happen until the end because you can't have much of an earthly existence with the heavens rolled-up.)***; and all their host shall fade away, as the leaf fadeth off the vine, and as a [fading] leaf from the fig-tree. (5) For my sword hath drunk its fill in heaven: behold, it shall come down upon <u>Edom</u>...*** "Edom" represents Esau. God is making a reference here to the battle between Jacob and Esau that is seen all the way through Scripture, and is seen even today in the natural. God said that He's going to bring His sword down upon Edom, the people of Esau, because they represent those people who have sold their birthright.

They belonged to God; they were of the seed of Abraham, but they sold their birthright. So God is here judging the people who, during the Tribulation, sold their birthright. They did not overcome.

(Isa.34:5) For my sword hath drunk its fill in heaven: behold, it shall come down upon Edom, and upon the people of my curse, to judgment. (6) The sword of the Lord is filled with blood, it is made fat with fatness, with the blood of lambs and goats, with the fat of the kidneys of rams; for the Lord hath a sacrifice in <u>Bozrah</u>, and a great slaughter in the land of <u>Edom</u>. "Edom" means "red" and symbolizes Esau's seed, and "Bozrah" means "sheep cote," so God is talking about the judgment of those who didn't keep their place in the Kingdom. He's talking about those who had a birthright to be a son of Abraham, but who despised their birthright and sold it instead. ***(7) And the wild-oxen shall come down with them, and the bullocks with the bulls: and their land shall be drunken with blood, and their dust made fat with fatness. (8) For the Lord hath a day of vengeance, a year of recompense for the cause of Zion. (9) And the streams of [Edom] shall be turned into pitch, and the dust thereof into brimstone, and the land thereof shall become burning pitch. (10) It shall not be quenched night nor day; the smoke thereof shall go up for ever...*** This is a type and shadow of what happens to those who have persecuted God's people. God will pour out His wrath on them in the days when the "flood" comes upon the earth, and "Noah" has entered into the "ark" to be preserved there, as the ark is lifted up by the flood.

We know from the Scriptures when this year begins. ***(Mat.24:29) But immediately after the <u>tribulation</u> of those days*** (This is speaking about the great end-time Tribulation.) ***the sun shall be darkened, and the moon shall not give her light, and the stars shall fall from heaven, and the powers of the heavens shall be shaken: (30) and then shall appear the sign of the Son of man in heaven: and then shall all the tribes of the earth mourn, and they shall see the Son of man coming on the clouds of heaven with power and great glory. (31) And he shall send forth his angels with a great sound of a <u>trumpet</u>*** (That's the <u>last</u> trump {1 Corinthians 15:52; Revelation 11:15}.), ***and they shall gather together his elect from the four winds, from one end of heaven to the other.*** Notice in the text he says <u>after</u> the tribulation, so <u>after</u> the seven years, the sun and the moon will be darkened and <u>then</u> He will gather His people. We find it also here. ***(Act.2:20) The sun shall be turned into darkness, And the moon into blood, <u>Before</u> the day of the Lord come, That great and notable [day].***

We're seeing exactly what we saw from the typology of Noah, where there were seven days and <u>then</u> there was a year of the flood. Now we see that after seven days, the sun and moon are darkened, and then after the sun and moon are darkened, we see the "day of the Lord" comes, which is the wrath that is poured out upon the wicked for how they have treated God's people. ***(1Th.4:17) Then <u>we</u> that are alive, <u>that are left</u>*** (These are those people who have overcome and have lived through the tribulation period until the time of the coming of the Lord.), ***shall together with <u>them</u>*** (These are the resurrected saints.)

be caught up in the clouds, to meet the Lord in the air: and so shall we ever be with the Lord. Isaiah later speaks again of the "day of the Lord," the "day of vengeance." ***(Isa.63:3) I have trodden the winepress alone; and of the peoples there was no man with me: yea I trod them in mine anger, and trampled them in my <u>wrath</u>*** (It's talking of the day of the Lord's wrath here.)***; and their lifeblood is sprinkled upon my garments, and I have stained all my raiment. (4) For the <u>day of vengeance</u> was in my heart, and the <u>year of my redeemed</u> is come.*** " The "<u>day</u> of vengeance" and the "<u>year</u> of God's redeemed" are the <u>same</u> year. As we saw, after the first 40 days of the day of God's wrath comes the day that God manifestly redeems us. We know that the Lord has already redeemed us by faith, but that's when He manifestly redeems His people from the earth. It's the day of His redeemed, or in other words, the day when the fullness of His redemption is received.

From What are We Redeemed?

God promises redemption. Everything we read in Psalm 91 is talking about escaping the judgment of the wars, and the hatred between the peoples, and the pestilences that are released at that time, and the missiles that fly by day, and so on and so forth. We know about this redemption, though many people don't (Luke 1:68-79). We've spoken about it before, but I'm going to mention it quickly because we need to be reminded. We need to stand upon these promises and speak them. God tells us here of this redemption when He says, "the year of my redeemed is come." From what are these people in the ark being redeemed? Well, they're being redeemed from a terrible war, where the nations are furiously releasing all of their weapons against one another, seeking to destroy their enemies before they lose the battle. God has put it in their hearts to do this and it's going to be a great slaughter. (Jeremiah 25:31-32). **(Jer.25:33) <u>And the slain of the Lord shall be at that day from one end of the earth even unto the other end of the earth</u>: they shall not be lamented, neither gathered, nor buried; they shall be dung upon the face of the ground.** It's going to be an astounding blood bath of the devil being released, who will just wreak havoc with those people who have rejected God's grace, rejected God's love, tormented His people, and so on.

We see in Luke where the Lord talks about the redemption and how broad it is. Zacharias, the father of John the Baptist, was filled with the Spirit and prophesied concerning both his son and the coming of Jesus. **(Luk.1:68) Blessed be the Lord, the God of Israel; For <u>he hath visited and wrought redemption for his people</u>.** The redemption has been manifested, saints; it has already been given. **(69) And hath raised up a horn of salvation for us In the house of <u>his servant David</u>** (Of course, this is speaking of Christ, and it also speaks of the end-time man-child, in whom Christ lives.) **(70) (As he spake by the mouth of his holy prophets that have been from of old), (71) <u>Salvation from our enemies</u>, and from the hand of all that hate us...** That means if you have God's redemption, and you have His salvation, then you're not going to go through the great and terrible day of the Lord. **(1Th.5:9) <u>For God appointed us not unto wrath</u>, but unto the obtaining of salvation through our Lord Jesus Christ.** Many people love to quote that verse, and it's true that we are not appointed unto "wrath." The "wrath" is that day of the Lord, the day that He pours out His wrath upon the wicked who have rejected His grace and rejected His Gospel and rejected His people. "Salvation from our enemies" is a part of redemption. His people are in the Ark of the secret place of the Most High. They're preserved from this terrible battle going on around them.

(Luk.1:71) Salvation from our enemies, and from the hand of all that hate us; (72) To show mercy towards our fathers, And to remember his holy covenant; (73) The oath which he sware unto Abraham our father, (74) To grant unto us that <u>we being delivered out of the hand of our enemies</u> Should serve him without fear. "Delivered out of the hand of our enemies" is a part of redemption, and this is going to be perfectly fulfilled in the days to come. The Lord told me that Psalm 91 represented a Passover for the saints. That Passover will be fulfilled corporately for the Church by their being in the Ark during these 40 days of the wrath of God. It's a Passover. It's a Psalm 91 preservation, where He says "A thousand shall fall at thy side, And ten thousand at thy right hand; [But] it shall not come nigh thee." Oh, praise God! He says that we <u>will</u> be delivered out of the hand of our enemies and that we <u>will</u> serve Him without fear. ***(Luk.1:74) To grant unto us that we being delivered out of the hand of our enemies Should serve him without fear, (75) In holiness and righteousness before him all our days.*** Then He prophesies of John the Baptist, who will go before His face. Praise God!

Saints, we're not taking anything away from Psalm 91; that's for you today and now. There have been and there are

God's Wondrous Protection and Provision   153

constantly many lesser fulfillments of this all the time. God's people, because of their faith, will be preserved through the midst of times when all the people around them are dying. The primary thing that puts you in the secret place of the Most High is your faith, **(Rom.10:10) *for with the heart man believeth unto righteousness; and with the mouth confession is made unto <u>salvation</u>.*** And "salvation" is what? "Salvation" is our <u>redemption</u>. An awesome fact is that we have a corporate fulfillment of this coming down the road in the not too-far-distant future. "It shall not come nigh thee." God's people will escape this death, this destruction at the hands of enemies because the Lord has performed this redemption, this deliverance.

We know that the Good News, the Gospel, is very broad. **(2Ti.1:10) *But hath now been manifested by the appearing of our Saviour <u>Christ Jesus</u>, <u>who abolished death</u>, <u>and brought life and immortality to light through the gospel</u>.*** As we've been seeing, the Good News is very broad, but many people put limits on it and don't really get the benefits that Christ paid for us to have. God has abolished death through Jesus Christ and He's brought life and immortality to light through the Gospel. We know that the people who enter into the Ark actually enter into immortality. The Greek word for "immortality" there is *aphtharsia* and it literally means "'deathlessness"; "indestructible, imperishable, incorruptible; hence: immortal." In other words, <u>the curse of death is gone</u>. They enter into immortality <u>before</u> they receive a new body because these people never die! They never die, like Joshua and Caleb in type. We've seen that Joshua and Caleb entered the Promised Land, but all their contemporaries died in the wilderness and only their children entered in (Numbers 14:28-32). They didn't get to enter in to the Promised Land, but Joshua and Caleb entered in, in their original, physical bodies. As for the others, in type only their "fruit" entered in, only their spiritual man entered in to the Promised Land while they died in the wilderness, but because Jesus abolished death, He "brought life and immortality to light." This is part of the Gospel.

Many people take what the Gospel says the way they want to take it, or they take it the way they are used to seeing it through their experience. If we take it the way the Bible teaches it, it may be something totally different, or it may be much broader and bigger than we think. God's promises are broad. The Lord paid the penalty for the curse of sin and death when He bore upon Himself the curse of sin and of death (Galatians 3:13-14, Romans 8:2). We've all experienced the Lord bearing our sins, taking them away, delivering us from them, but what about death? Is there a point in time when God will actually fulfill that, too? Yes. The Bible says, **(1Co.15:26) The <u>last</u> enemy that shall be abolished is death.** That is because the soul that sins must die (Ezekiel 18:20), and if you are sinning, you haven't overcome all the other enemies yet (Romans 8:12-13). The Lord is leading us that way, and there will be a time when people who are alive and remain will never die (1 Thessalonians 4:17).

Everything that we pray for has a foundation in the Sacrifice. We just saw that we've been redeemed from the curse of sin and redeemed from the curse of death, which is the last enemy to be overcome, but that's about to be fulfilled in these last days. ***(Joh.11:25) Jesus said unto her, I am the resurrection and the life: he that believeth on me, though he die, yet shall he live*** (So He's talking about physical death and coming back one day)*; **(26) and whosoever liveth and believeth on me shall <u>never die</u>. <u>Believest thou this</u>?** Is Jesus still talking about physical death? Yes. He's not going to deceive us here. He's not going to just switch words on us in the middle of a text. He's telling us very plainly that if we live and believe on Him, we shall <u>never</u> die.

"<u>Believest thou this</u>?" That's the question. Not everybody believes it is their right to have a Psalm 91 deliverance from this terrible curse of death that's going to come upon the whole world. The entire curse is going to be fulfilled upon the world, but God is going to have a people that are going to escape from the whole curse because they <u>believe</u> what the <u>Bible</u> says. They believe what the Bible says and not just in the limitations of what they've been taught or may have experienced in their past. What we're about to see, the miraculous salvations and deliverances that are going to be received, we've never experienced in the past. Glory to God! I know some people are thinking, "Ha! You're crazy, David." That's okay with me; you're free to believe what you want to believe, but if you can receive it, the Lord has redeemed us from <u>all</u> of the curse. If you say, "You know, David, I haven't seen any of those people around." Well, you have seen people around you who haven't died, and the Lord said that in these days, in this morning of the third day, or the morning of the seventh day, depending upon from which Adam you are counting, all these things will be fulfilled (Hosea 6:2-3). Hallelujah!

(Psa.91:8) Only with thine eyes shalt thou behold, And see the reward of the wicked. Certainly that promise was fulfilled by Noah and his family in the ark. They looked out the window and witnessed the curse of death coming upon all mankind. They saw "the reward of the wicked." Some people think that they are going to fly away and never have to see this, but that's not going to happen because it's not according to Scripture. Remember that the last enemy to be conquered is death, and that's not going to happen seven years before the end. As you can see, they entered the ark seven days before the rain of destruction began, and in type, those seven days are the seven years before the day of the Lord's wrath. Then they remained on the earth in the ark for forty days before they were lifted up. Those forty days are forty days into the last year, which we've learned is the great and terrible day of the Lord's wrath, so we will get to see the beginning of this destruction. If you live that long, you will get to see it. ***(Psa.91:9) For thou, O Lord, art my refuge! Thou hast made the Most High thy habitation.*** We make the Most High our "habitation" by believing in our heart and confessing with our mouth. This is where salvation comes from. "For thou O Lord, art my refuge!" That's a confession and it's the way we enter into this deliverance, by faith. It's a confession that is first in your mind and then comes out of your mouth. "Thou hast made the Most High thy habitation."

    I'd like to briefly look at a few other psalms that speak about deliverance from enemies and living through this time when enemies are everywhere, especially for Christians. ***(Psa.25:19) Consider mine enemies, for they are many…*** We've never had as many enemies as we are about to have in this world. Jesus said, ***(Mat.24:9) Then shall they deliver you up unto tribulation, and shall kill you: and <u>ye shall be hated of all the nations for my name's sake</u>. (10) And then shall*** *many stumble, and shall deliver up one another, and shall hate one another.* In other words, because His Name will be manifested in us, His Nature, Character, and Authority, we're going to have many enemies. Can God protect you from many enemies? Yes, we just saw it. *(Psa.25:19) Consider mine enemies, for they are many; And they hate me with cruel hatred. (20) Oh keep my soul, and deliver me: Let me not be put to shame, for I take refuge in thee. (21) <u>Let integrity and uprightness preserve me</u>...* Integrity and uprightness are part of this preservation, folks. You can't escape it. Some people think it's just faith, but you can't have faith without boldness in your righteousness, without walking in righteousness and integrity. *(1Jn.3:21) Beloved, if our heart condemn us not, we have boldness toward God; (22) and whatsoever we ask we receive of him, because we keep his commandments and do the things that are pleasing in his sight.*

(Psa.25:21) Let integrity and uprightness preserve me, For I wait for thee. (22) Redeem Israel, O God, Out of <u>all</u> of his troubles. That gives you another idea of what redemption actually is. We are redeemed from the curse, including the curse of the hatred of all mankind that's going to come against the Christians in these days. It's going to be a supernatural curse, too. It's not at all natural. People won't be able to reason it or understand it because it's going to be a supernatural, demonic takeover of planet earth and its people. *(Rev.18:2) And he cried with a mighty voice, saying, Fallen, fallen is Babylon the great, and is become a <u>habitation of demons</u>, <u>and a hold of every unclean spirit</u>, and a hold of every unclean and hateful bird.*

(Psa.27:2) When evil-doers came upon me to eat up my flesh, [Even] mine adversaries and my foes, they stumbled and fell. (3) Though a <u>host should encamp against me</u> (Or, "an army encamp against me."), ***<u>My heart shall not fear</u>: Though war should rise against me, Even then will I be confident.*** Wow! "My heart shall not fear." That's the Word of the Lord. Ask the Lord to give you a fearless heart in the midst of anything that you can see with your eyes. The Lord will supernaturally preserve the faith in your heart, even in the midst of much trouble and tribulation. Is God able to do this? Absolutely. I hear so many people say that all their Christian life they thought Psalm 91 wasn't for today, that it was for the Millennium or some silly thing like that, but too many people have depended upon its promises and have been preserved. Many, many times, warriors in the military have claimed Psalm 91 and have been supernaturally preserved. They pass Psalm 91 around in the military, folks, not that the promises aren't all throughout the Bible, but they are certainly concentrated very well right here. Thank You, Father!

(Psa.91:10) There shall no evil befall thee, Neither shall any plague come nigh thy tent. That also sounds very much like this promise. ***(Exo.12:13) ... And when I see the blood, I will pass over you, and there shall no plague be upon you to destroy you, when I smite the land of Egypt.*** So God says, "There shall no evil befall thee, Neither shall any plague come nigh thy tent." Believe it! Confess it! Speak it! Claim it as <u>yours</u>. This is a Psalm 91 Passover that we're talking about here. Of course, this Psalm 91 Passover is obviously a promise for you when you need it, but it's also going to have a corporate end-time fulfillment, too. **(11) <u>For he will give his angels charge over thee</u>, To keep thee in all thy ways. (12) They shall bear thee up in their hands, Lest thou dash thy foot against a stone.** The job of God's angels is to preserve the saints and minister to the saints.

The angels fulfill God's Will. **(Psa.103:19) The Lord hath established his throne in the heavens; And his kingdom ruleth over all. (20) Bless the Lord, ye <u>his angels</u>, That are mighty in strength, <u>that fulfil his word</u>** (Where do they "fulfil his word"? <u>Here</u>, on the earth.), **Hearkening unto the voice of his word.** And the Bible also says, **(Heb.1:14) Are they not all ministering spirits, sent forth to do service for the sake of them that shall inherit <u>salvation</u>?** Now we know what salvation is and we've discovered that it's very, very broad. The Greek word for "salvation" is *soteria* and the word for "saved" is *sozo*. They are used in the Bible to cover not just salvation of the soul, but salvation of the physical body and salvation from circumstances. These ministering spirits are sent forth to serve, or to do service for, those who are to inherit the salvation. It is inherited, of course, through our faith. We believe Psalm 91. The angels are not going to protect a person who will not believe Psalm 91.

Even the devil quoted Psalm 91 when he tempted Jesus to throw Himself down from the wing of the Temple, saying the angels would bear Him up and not let Him dash a foot against a stone (Matthew 4:6). You may point out, "But they didn't protect Jesus from the Cross." Well, that's because He was the Sacrifice. He bore the curse upon Himself. Of course, Jesus did go to His Cross, and that is so that we wouldn't have to go to a physical cross, but we do have to go to our spiritual cross. ***(Gal.2:20) I have been crucified with Christ; and it is no longer I that live, but Christ living in me: and that [life] which I now live in the flesh I live in faith, [the faith] which is in the Son of God, who loved me, and gave himself up for me.*** We have to lose our life to gain our life. ***(Mat.16:25) For whosoever would save his life shall lose it: and whosoever shall lose his life for my sake shall find it.*** We have to be crucified with Christ in order to enter in to all that He is, because this old man is our enemy. As a matter of fact, this old man that is born from below is the most important enemy that we must conquer. The new man that is born from above (John 3:3, 8:23) is the eternal creature that is in the Image of Jesus Christ. Oh glory!

The Word is in Us

(Psa.103:20) Bless the Lord, ye his angels, That are mighty in strength, that fulfil his word, <u>Hearkening unto the voice of his word</u>. The angels listen for the Word of the Lord. Now most people probably think that's talking about the Word of the Lord from heaven, but the Word of the Lord is in <u>us</u>, and we should be speaking the Word of the Lord (1 Peter 4:11). If we are not speaking the Word of the Lord, we are binding His angels from doing this work of ministering salvation to us (Matthew 18:18). Salvation comes through faith, and faith better be coming out of our mouth in any circumstances such as those in Psalm 91. We need to be speaking God's salvation and God's promises out of our mouth. When we do, the angels hearken unto the voice of that Word and they go forth to do service for them that are heirs of salvation.

Why are they heirs of salvation? They are heirs of salvation because they're repenting of their sins, walking in holiness, speaking their faith. They're believing for <u>all</u> the awesome promises given them in the Word of God.

(Psa.103:21) Bless the Lord, all ye his hosts, Ye ministers of his, that do his pleasure. There are times we may think that we're dealing directly with the Lord when, instead, we're dealing with His angels that are fulfilling His Word. Angels are perfect representatives of His; they're perfect prophets because when they speak to you, it is the Lord Who speaks to you. When Moses spoke with the Lord in the burning bush (Exodus 3:2), it was a "perfect prophet," an angel, who was speaking to Moses (Exodus 3:2). This angel was called "the angel of His presence." (Exodus 23:20, 33:14-15; Isaiah 63:9). **(Psa.103:21) Bless the Lord, <u>all ye his hosts</u>** (That is the armies of His angels.)**, Ye <u>ministers</u> of his** (They "minister," they "bring to pass," His Word.)**, that do his pleasure.** The angels are continually waiting to hear the Word of God so that they can fulfill it. That means it behooves us to <u>speak in agreement</u> with the Word of God so that we don't hinder what they do. If we confess Jesus before men, He will confess us before the Father and before the angels. (Luke 12:8-9, Matthew 10:32-33) The word "confess" means "to speak the same as." When <u>we</u> speak the same as Jesus Christ, when <u>we</u> confess the promises of God, the angels have authority from the Lord to go forth and do likewise. So it's very important "to speak the same as" because we don't want to have an unemployed angel. We want to put that angel to work. And when the Lord promises that He'll give His angels charge over us to keep us in all of our ways, He means <u>all</u> of our ways.

(Psa.91:11) For he will give his angels charge over thee, To keep thee in <u>all</u> thy ways. That's such an awesome promise! They won't let you have even a little accident when this is being fulfilled. ***(12) They shall bear thee up in their hands, Lest thou dash thy foot against a stone. (13) Thou shalt tread upon the lion and adder: The young lion and the <u>serpent</u> shalt thou trample under foot.*** God has given us authority over the serpents! Praise His Name! Remember we were told, ***(Luk.10:17) And the seventy returned with joy, saying, Lord, even the demons are subject unto us in thy name. (18) And he said unto them, I beheld Satan fallen as lightning from heaven. (19) Behold, I have given you <u>authority to tread upon serpents and scorpions</u>, and over all the power of the enemy: and <u>nothing shall in any wise hurt you</u>.*** There it is, Psalm 91, right there: "nothing shall in any wise hurt you" and "authority to tread on serpents and scorpions." ***(20) Nevertheless in this rejoice not, that the <u>spirits are subject unto you</u>*** (Notice that the "serpents" and "scorpions" are <u>spirits</u> which are subject unto you.)***; but rejoice that your names are written in heaven.***

The Greek word for scorpions is *skorpios* and the Lord showed me it's used in several ways in the Scriptures. One example is, ***(Luk.11:23) He that is not with me is against me; and he that gathereth not with me <u>scattereth</u>.*** That word "scattereth" is the word *skorpizó*, which is another rendering of *skorpios*. *Skorpizó* means "to penetrate and put to flight." It's what the Lord did when He sent for His hornets to scatter the Canaanites, to cause them to be fearful and run from the Israelites (Exodus

23:28-30). Hornets are pretty fearful because they have a sting that feels like fire and they're almost impossible to swat away. At any rate, we are to "tread upon serpents and scorpions," which are two different kinds of demon spirits that make war against us. A serpent has its poison in its head, and usually a serpent spirit has something to do with deception or delusion. A scorpion has its poison in its tail, and a scorpion spirit has to do with fear, panic, rejection, anxiety, guilt, shame, unbelief, and so on. Serpent spirits can manifest as fortune telling; that happened with the soothsaying maid, who had a spirit, a "python," as it says in the original Greek (Acts 16:16). A "python" is a spirit of divination, which is a spirit of deception or delusion, a spirit of false prophesy. There are Christians today who think they have a gift of prophesy but it is a deceiving spirit. The venom in the head has to do with knowledge, false knowledge, deception, and delusion. We are supposed to exercise authority over these spirits because God has given us victory over them. That's part of our Psalm 91 heritage.

(Psa.91:14) Because he hath set his love upon me, therefore will I deliver him... Do you love the Lord? That will be proven. Jesus said, **(Joh.14:15) If ye love me, ye will keep my commandments.** And, **(Joh.14:23) ... If a man love me, he will keep my word: and my Father will love him, and we will come unto him, and make our abode with him.** Is it more important to you to keep His commandments than to serve your flesh and keep the old man alive? It should be, and it will be proven in the days ahead. That's what a "tribulation" is: It's a trial for God's people. We're going to face manifold trials in the days ahead (1 Peter 1:6) to see whether we're going to count the cost and give up the old life. ***(Psa.91:14) Because he hath set his love upon me, therefore will I deliver him: I will set him on high, because he hath known my <u>name</u>.*** This is a part of His provision of delivering God's people from the curse of this world. I will set him on high because "he hath known my name." You know, the Bible says, ***(Pro.18:10) <u>The name of the Lord is a strong tower</u>; The righteous runneth into it, and is <u>safe</u>.*** The Hebrew word there for "safe" is *sagab* and it actually means "exalted; to be (inaccessibly) high." Do you know the Name of the Lord? "Name" means "nature, character, and authority" in both the Greek and Hebrew. There are many people who have made up their own "Jesus," but he can't save. That's the whole point. If you do have a "Jesus" of your own making and you put your faith in him, then you are putting your faith in an idol. Idols cannot save. It doesn't matter if you call your idol "Jesus"; it cannot save you.

Another Jesus

Many people put their trust in a "Jesus" that does not exist and, of course, then the real Jesus can't answer, because if He did, He would be confirming a lie. When those people exercise their faith in this "Jesus" that they've created for themselves, he fails them because he's not the real Jesus. They don't have the real Name, the real Nature, Character, and Authority. If you want to be saved, it's important to make sure that your Jesus is the Jesus of the Bible, because no other "Jesus" can save. As a matter of fact, that's idolatry, and the Lord warns us over and over that people's idols cannot save them (Exodus 34:17; 1 Kings 14:9,16:33; etc.) Their idols won't save them today just as their idols didn't save them back then. Many deceiving spirits out there have taken over Christians (1 Timothy 4:1-2), and they believe these spirits are God Himself, but this is a delusion. When they put their faith in such a spirit, that spirit will fail them.

The True God Delivers

(Psa.91:14) Because he hath set his love upon me, therefore will I deliver him: I will set him on high, because he hath known <u>my name</u>. (15) <u>He shall call upon me</u>, <u>and I will answer him</u>... This is a person who <u>knows</u> the Name of the Lord. God says of them, "He shall call upon me, and I will answer him." If you are not trusting in God to be your Savior, then you don't yet know the true nature of His Name, **(Heb.11:6) ...for he that cometh to God must believe that he is, and [that] he is a rewarder of them that seek after him.** When you <u>seek</u> after the Lord, you <u>will</u> become familiar with the true Nature of God through the Scriptures so that you can put your trust in Him. That's how you come to know His Name and then you can call upon Him and He will answer you. **(Psa.91:15) He shall call upon me, and I will answer him; I will be with him in trouble: I will deliver him** (Not everybody gets delivered, but God promises that He will deliver those who abide in the secret place of the Most High, those who know His Name.)**, and honor him.** These are the righteous, and Scripture says that they will not be put to shame (Romans 10:11). They have put their trust in Him and they will not be put to shame. Praise be to God! That's another awesome promise! The devil often tempts us with the thought that we're going to be put to shame, that God is going to fail us, but the Lord has promised that He will be our Deliverer and our Provider. He will honor our faith. He will honor us.

(Psa.91:16) With <u>long life</u> will I satisfy him (Yes, the longest life. As a matter of fact, eternal life.)**, And show him my salvation.** Oh praise Him! We need to know how big God's salvation really is, we need to know that it covers <u>all</u> of the curses of this earth. We need to learn to do preventative maintenance by <u>claiming</u> these promises. Pray Psalm 91. I do a lot of studying the Word, and I pray as I read. I run across things that make me say, "Yep, I want that," and I pray for it. As I read, it reminds me of things to pray for. I do a lot of praying with my Bible because I see things that either I need, or people around me need, and I pray them. I do my very best to hold fast that <u>confession</u> of my hope.

Well, what do you think? Do you want God's inoculations? Or do you want man's inoculations? I've thought many times that multitudes of people are going to be sick in this world because they put their trust in men and their vaccines. There are so many pestilences coming upon the world, even new pestilences engineered by man, and you can't get vaccinated every time a new version of this or that comes out. The pharmaceutical companies say that it's safe to take multiple vaccines at the same time, but they can't hide that there are terrible side-effects and some people die. Pretty soon, folks, this habit of trusting in man is going to be proven to be a curse. Their vaccines will kill you, but if you put your trust in the Lord, you can't lose.

God's "vaccine" covers it all, folks. It covers it all. If <u>you</u> abide in the secret place of the Most High, God will make sure that no pestilence, no plague, will come "nigh thy tent." Praise God! Fill yourself with the Word of the Lord and His promises, and you'll be prepared for these days that are coming, because God will preserve you. You'll be a witness and a testimony to the people around you. You'll be an encouragement and a strengthening unto them. You'll be able to pass on the power of the Lord to them and save many who can't save themselves. All glory to You, Father!

Father, in the Name of Jesus, we ask you, Lord, that Your power and anointing be upon all those who are reading this. Let Your Word be alive in their hearts. Lord, we fill up these clay vessels with the Word of God, the Water of God, and trust You will turn it into the wine of the Life and the Blood of Jesus Christ. Lord, let His Life be in us to overcome anything that we will be faced with in this world. Oh, praise be to God! Thank You so much, Father. Thank you for Your utter and complete protection of Psalm 91, Your Passover Lamb of Jesus Christ, which we eat daily. Today, we've eaten a portion of the Manna that came down out of heaven that gives life to the world. You said You are going to try us to see if we'll eat our portion every day and that's what we dearly need to do, Lord. We need to eat our portion every day to inoculate us from the curses of this world, the plagues of this world, the pestilences of this world, and the other judgments that Psalm 91 speaks about. Thank You, Father, thank You for Your wondrous provision. We receive it today, in Jesus' Name.

CHAPTER SEVEN

Anxiety and Fear, Part 1

Casting Down Anxiety

Lord, precious Father, we thank You so much for Your grace today and our fellowship with the brethren. Lord, give us Your Presence today, Your powerful Presence. Give us Your anointing. Lord, encourage the saints and take all fear and anxiety out of our hearts concerning the days to come. We know that You have awesome, tremendous plans for us and we want Your peace in every place that we go. You taught us in Isaiah 26:3, Lord, that **Thou wilt keep [him] in perfect peace, [whose] mind [is] stayed [on thee]; because he trusteth in thee.** Keep our minds upon You, Lord, and on the Word of God, so we will be stable. Father, help us to stand on the Rock concerning the things that we see and hear. Let them not cause us to waver, let us not be moved by anything but Your Word, Lord. We ask for this grace in Jesus' Name, amen.

Folks, there are some mighty shakings of God coming (Hebrews 12:26-29). You're going to see things that you never thought you would see in this world, but the Lord doesn't want us to be troubled about it. It's all part of His plan. He is a sovereign God and He works all things after the counsel of His Own Will. *(Eph.1:11) In whom also we were made a heritage, having been foreordained according to the purpose of him <u>who worketh all things after the counsel of his will</u>.* And, as the Bible also says, *(Joh.3:27) ... <u>A man can receive nothing, except it have been given him from heav-</u>*

en. God is the only One Who "doeth according to his will." *(Dan.4:35) And all the inhabitants of the earth are reputed as nothing; and <u>he doeth according to his will</u> in the army of heaven, and among the inhabitants of the earth; and none can stay his hand, or say unto him, What doest thou?* He reigns in the heavens and upon the earth. *(1Ch.16:31) Let the heavens be glad, and let the earth rejoice; And let them say among the nations, <u>the Lord reigneth</u>.* So we can trust in Him.

These shakings are coming in order to bring many people into the Kingdom, and yet, we don't want to be anxious or fearful concerning these things. We want to be at peace. We want to be able to be used of God when these things happen, but we are totally useless to God if we have anxiety or fear, and the devil knows that. Yes, the devil is about to make great war on the saints but those who walk by faith, those who draw close to the Lord, those who depend upon Him even for their faith and their grace, have nothing to worry about. Through these great shakings, God is going to weed out the apostates from among His true people. Only those who have received the gift from God to want to walk with Him will remain.

You know, when Jesus sent the disciples and the seventy out, it was on-the-job training for them. The Lord showed me that this was a foretaste, a foreshadowing, of what's going to happen in our day in the beginning of the tribulation period. That's because history repeats. *(Ecc.1:9) That which hath been is that which shall be; and that which hath been done is that which shall be done: and there is no new thing under the sun.* We are coming into a great time of grace, and the Lord is going to appear. He is going to be manifested in His people. ***(Col.1:26) [Even] the mystery which hath been hid for ages and generations: but now hath it been manifested to his saints, (27) to whom God was pleased to make known what is the riches of the glory of this mystery among the Gentiles, which is <u>Christ in you</u>, <u>the hope of glory</u>: (28) whom we proclaim, admonishing every man and teaching every man in all wisdom, that we may present every man perfect in Christ.*** He is going to be manifested as "Christ in you, the hope of glory," and His Firstfruits are going to be able to do the same things that Jesus did in raising-up disciples, the sending forth two-by-two, and so on; all this will be repeated. Great and wondrous things are going to happen. Oh, praise the Lord!

(Luk.10:17) And the seventy returned with joy, saying, Lord, even the demons are subject unto us in thy name. Some of you know this already, but the overwhelming majority of Christianity does not. As a matter of fact, even the overwhelming majority of God's elect don't yet know this, but they will. They will come out (Isaiah 52:11; John 10:3; 2 Corinthians 6:17), they will be led, they will be disciples, and then they will shake the world (Haggai 2:6; Acts 17:6; Hebrews 12:26-27). So the seventy were overjoyed to find out that the demons were subject to them. Jesus told His disciples, ***(Mar.16:17) And these signs shall accompany them that believe: in my name shall they cast out demons...*** We have been given <u>authority</u> over demon powers, saints, and it is a joyous thing to see people set free, but how do we defend ourselves against these demons? The attacks are coming. The warfare is about to go forth against the saints, yet God's people, those who walk by faith, will have nothing to worry about. I'd like to share with you from Luke about fear and anxiety. Of course, once the Lord has put His Word in your heart and you have some experience walking in that Word, it is very hard for fear and anxiety to come into your heart. This is what God wants to do; He wants to prepare us for the things to come. I know that some people won't be prepared. They will be shocked and they will be fearful, however, because of that fear, they will run to the Lord for refuge and then God will teach them how to walk in peace and rest.

(Luk.10:18) And he said unto them, I beheld Satan fallen as lightning from heaven. (19) Behold, I have given you authority to tread upon serpents and scorpions, and over all the power of the enemy: and nothing shall in any wise hurt you. (20) Nevertheless in this rejoice not, that the spirits are subject unto you; but rejoice that your names are written in heaven. We see they came back rejoicing that the demons were subject to them, and then Jesus mentions that He has given them authority to tread upon "serpents" and "scorpions." "Serpents" and "scorpions" here represent two different kinds of the spirits over which they were exercising their authority. I want to explain that to you because it has a lot of bearing on anxiety and fear and how to deal with it.

Serpent Spirits

First I need to point out to you that there are "serpent" spirits, but I am not going to go deep into this. I have taught on this before and I want to talk more about anxiety and fear. ***(Act.16:16) And it came to pass, as we were going to the place of prayer, that a certain maid having a <u>spirit of divination</u> met us, who brought her masters much gain by soothsaying. (17) The same following after Paul and us cried out, saying, These men are servants of the Most High God, who proclaim unto you the way of salvation. (18) And this she did for many days. But Paul, being sore troubled, turned and said to the spirit, I charge thee in the name of Jesus Christ to come out of her. And it came out that very hour.*** A "spirit of divination" is a spirit of false prophecy, and if we look at the original Greek words there, we find that they mean a "spirit of python." In other words, a spirit of divination is a serpent spirit, and a big one. As you know, serpents that are poisonous carry their poison in their <u>heads</u>. One of the reasons the Lord pointed this out to me is because serpent spirits are deceiving spirits, and so they war with your <u>mind</u>. False prophecy does that, along with all the other serpent spirits. They bring deception to mankind.

Scorpion Spirits

However, it is the second group, the "scorpions," that I want to deal with here. Jesus said, "I have given you authority to <u>tread</u> upon serpents and scorpions." "Tread" means to "put them under your feet, under your authority, under your dominion." The word "scorpions" in the Greek, is *skorpios* and it's where we get our English word "scorpion." As Jesus was making war against the demon powers, He was teaching His disciples how to make war against the demon powers. ***(Luk.11:17) ... Every kingdom divid-***

ed against itself is brought to desolation; and a house [divided] against a house falleth. (18) And if Satan also is divided against himself, how shall his kingdom stand? because ye say that I cast out demons by Beelzebub. (19) And if I by Beelzebub cast out demons, by whom do your sons cast them out? therefore shall they be your judges. (20) But if I by the finger of God cast out demons, then is the kingdom of God come upon you. Obviously, Satan does not cast out Satan; it is only the Kingdom of God that gives deliverance from Satan and his demons. *(21) When the strong [man] fully armed guardeth his own court, his goods are at peace: (22) but when a stronger than he shall come upon him, and overcome him, he taketh from him his whole armor wherein he trusted, and divideth his spoils.* And we know that Jesus was stronger than the "strong man." He conquered the devil, and when He passed His authority on to His disciples, He was giving us authority over all the power of the enemy. He was dividing the spoils.

We are plundering the devil's kingdom when we preach the Gospel to someone and they believe it. When that happens, they are delivered out of the devil's kingdom and into the Kingdom of God. The same thing happens when we heal the sick, and when we cast out demons, and so on. That's our job, folks; we all have a job to do in plundering the devil's kingdom. *(Luk.11:23) He that is not with me is against me; and he that gathereth not with me scattereth.* We need to be on the Lord's side. He ordained us, He raised us up, and He wants us all to have a part in this. No matter where we are or what we are doing, we work for the Kingdom of God and we represent the

King. We are ambassadors of Christ (2 Corinthians 5:20). We speak for Him in this world. We go forth to do His works in this world. Jesus said, *(Mar.16:17) And these signs <u>shall</u> accompany them that believe: in my name shall they cast out demons; they shall speak with new tongues; (18) they shall take up serpents, and if they drink any deadly thing, it shall in no wise hurt them; they shall lay hands on the sick, and they shall recover.* These things "<u>shall</u> accompany them that believe." If <u>you</u> are a believer, <u>you</u> have a right to all the gifts of the Spirit. If <u>you</u> are a believer, <u>you</u> have a right to be doing the work of God by healing the sick, casting out devils, speaking in tongues, and so on and so forth.

"He that gathereth not with me scattereth." I have pointed out before that the word "scattereth" here is the Greek word *skorpizo*, and it means "to penetrate and put to flight." There are some small creatures that sometimes frighten people more than big creatures, and a scorpion is a very small creature, but it is frightening because people know the pain, the trouble, and the poison that can come from it. When the Israelites were going into their Promised Land, God spoke to them, saying, *(Exo.23:28) And I will send the hornet before thee, which shall drive out the Hivite, the Canaanite, and the Hittite, from before thee.* A hornet is another very small creature, but it has a sting in its tail, just like the scorpion. The poison is in its tail, not in its head, and when it goes forth, it can put a lot of people to flight. Of course, God was using the hornet as a type and a shadow, in the same way He was using it here for the scorpion to penetrate and put to flight. Your defense against this is to take up *(Eph.6:16) ... the shield of faith, wherewith ye shall be able*

to quench all the fiery darts of the evil [one]. You need the shield of faith whenever you're attacked by these scorpion spirits because their job is to cause you to run, and they do a very good job of it. The Lord has taught me that certain of these scorpion spirits cause God's people to run from the battle, to give-up in the face of the enemy. Two of the big ones are spirits of anxiety and fear, but others are spirits of guilt, spirits of rejection, spirits of shame, and spirits of unbelief. They cause God's people not to take up their sword of the spirit, the shield of faith, the helmet of salvation, and so on and so forth to conquer the enemy (Ephesians 6:10-17). Knowledge of the Word of God and understanding who we are in Christ, understanding that He <u>has</u> delivered us, gives us power over them. If we are not with Jesus, we are against Him. If we are not gathering with Him, then <u>we</u> are scattered.

Plunder or Be Plundered

Of course, if you are not plundering Satan's kingdom, that means Satan is plundering you. You can't have it both ways; it is one way or the other. The Lord has given us the victory in Jesus Christ, we know that. We know because of the Sacrifice that He gave, that we have been given victory. He said, ***(Joh.16:33) These things have I spoken unto you, that in me ye may have peace. In the world ye have tribulation: but <u>be of good cheer</u>; <u>I have overcome the world</u>.*** Jesus conquered the devil, the evil one, He conquered sin, He conquered the curse, He conquered sickness; He conquered it <u>all</u> at the Cross. We have already studied the real Good News that gives us authority and power over the devil. [Editor's Note: Our book,

The Real Good News, is available without charge from ubm1.org as a PDF.] We should be able to defend ourselves against the fear and anxiety that is going to attack many people when they see the judgments that are coming upon this world. It is quite normal and natural for the wicked to run and to be fearful and to be moved by what they see and what they hear, but not for us. **(Pro.28:1) The wicked flee when no man pursueth; But the righteous are bold as a lion.** We need to hold fast that bold faith that the Lord has given to us (Romans 3:22; Ephesians 3:12; Hebrews 10:35; etc.)

Unforgivness Brings the Tormentors

You should know that there are some things that will totally take away your defense against these demon spirits, and one of the major ones that I have seen is unforgiveness. Having unforgiveness, or one of its relatives such as bitterness or judgment toward anybody, is what delivers many of God's people over to the power of these demons. [Editor's Note: Our book, *The Curse of Unforgiveness*, is available without charge from ubm1.org as a PDF.] Jesus warned us, **(Mat.18:34) And his lord was wroth, and <u>delivered him to the tormentors</u>, till he should pay all that was due. (35) So shall also my heavenly Father do unto you, if ye forgive not every one his brother from your hearts.** If we don't forgive our brother from the heart, the Father will turn us over to the tormentors until we pay our own debt. It's sad but many of God's people don't realize that they're laboring under these tormenting demons. They can't get victory, they can't overcome, they have no confidence, they have no gift of faith, yet they don't understand that it's because they're holding on to unforgiveness, bitterness, and judgment against their brothers. Jesus is not a liar. He said the Father will turn you over to the tormentors.

If we want to have boldness before God, one thing that we have to do, folks, is to make sure that we have a clean conscience. ***(1Jn.3:21) Beloved, <u>if our heart condemn us not</u>, <u>we have boldness toward God</u>; (22) and <u>whatsoever we ask we receive of him</u>*** (Now that's a place of safety! We don't have to worry about a thing; we just ask, and God answers.)***, because we <u>keep his commandments</u> and <u>do the things that are pleasing in his sight</u>.*** In other words, we have a clean conscience. This should put the fear of the Lord in you, not the fear of anybody else. The only One we have to please is the Lord Himself. If you want to be ready for the things that are coming at you down the road, then you need to have a clean conscience because the devil is going to send in his big guns of fear and anxiety to lead the pack. Usually what happens is people see or hear something and all of a sudden, the devil is there to penetrate and to put to flight. He is there to attack. That is when we need to be full of the boldness of the Lord and realize we are dealing with the enemy. This is not our mind; this is the devil attacking our mind, trying to bring us down so that we will be totally useless in this battle.

Fear is Evil

One important thing that we have to understand is that fear is sin. Many times people think fear is a weakness in them. They think they just don't have the faith that they need, but the Bible calls this "an evil heart of unbelief." **(Heb.3:12) Take heed, brethren, lest haply there shall be in any one of you an evil heart of unbelief, in falling away from the living God.** And we are told, **(Rev.21:8) But for the <u>fearful</u>, <u>and unbelieving</u>** (So it is a sin that's thrown in there with all of the other sins.)**, and abominable, and murderers, and fornicators, and sorcerers, and idolaters, and all liars, their part [shall be] in the lake that burneth with fire and brimstone; which is the second death.** When you are tempted with fear and anxiety, you should deal with that as sin. Many people just give in to fear, but the Bible says, **(2Ti.1:7) For <u>God gave us not a spirit of fearfulness</u>; but of power and love and discipline.** When that spirit of fear comes, it is of the devil. When that spirit comes, it is in order to manipulate us and to move us to react to the situation, instead of acting according to what the Word of God says. The devil wants to put us to flight before him so that he can continue to plunder us.

(Luk.10:19) Behold, <u>I have given you authority</u> (That includes dominion over anxiety and fear.) **to tread upon serpents and scorpions, and <u>over all the power of the enemy</u>: <u>and nothing shall in any wise hurt you</u>.** We need to be bold in our faith because we have been given authority over the devil in everything and "nothing shall in any wise hurt" us. Does that verse actually mean that? Of course it does! It means that nothing shall in any wise hurt us, but that promise is only effectual when you mix it with faith (Hebrews chapters 3 and 4). **(Heb.4:1) Let us fear therefore, lest haply, a promise being left of entering into his rest, any one of you should seem to have come short of it. (2) For**

indeed we have had good tidings preached unto us, even as also they: <u>but the word of hearing did not profit them, because it was not united by faith with them that heard</u>.

    We know from God's word that these shakings are going to come. **(Heb.12:26) Whose voice then shook the earth: but now he hath promised, saying, Yet once more will I make to tremble not the earth only, but also the heaven. (27) And this [word], Yet once more, signifieth the removing of those things that are shaken, as of things that have been made, that those things which are not shaken may remain. (28) Wherefore, receiving a kingdom that cannot be shaken, let us have grace, whereby we may offer service well-pleasing to God with reverence and awe: (29) for our God is a consuming fire.** God is going to bring down this world through these great shakings and He is going to bring shakings in the lives of His people. Events will occur that you and I have never seen on this earth. In fact, things that have never happened before are going to happen and they're going to put the fear of God in His elect. However, they're going to put the fear of the devil, the fear of the curse, and the fear of the things that are coming upon the world in the hearts of the wicked. There will be **(Luk.21:26KJV) Men's hearts failing them for fear, and for looking after those things which are coming on the earth: for the powers of heaven shall be shaken.** Only God's elect are going to have His patience and His peace in the midst of this. I am not saying they are going to have it all of a sudden and at the beginning, but they are all going to grow into it. They're all going to understand what it is to serve the Lord. They're all going to be highly motivated because of the things that are coming upon the world.

Yes, these shakings are coming but we need to call fear and anxiety what God calls them, we need to call them "sin." God has given us a deliverance from this, ***(Heb.10:14) For by one offering he hath perfected for ever them that are sanctified.*** We can count on it because God has delivered us from <u>all</u> sin. ***(Joh.1:29) ... Behold, the Lamb of God, that <u>taketh away the sin</u> of the world!*** Jesus took away our sin. Jesus took away fear and anxiety. We don't have to put up with it because He did that, therefore we can partake of the peace of God in the midst of great destructions upon this world. ***(Isa.26:3) Thou wilt keep [him] in perfect peace, [whose] mind [is] stayed on [thee]; because he trusteth in thee.*** Those destructions are coming and they are coming fast and so we need to be prepared. It is a trick of the devil to immediately show up with fear and anxiety whenever something like this happens, and you need to cast it down. We are children of the King and we are here for His purpose, not for the purpose of the world. What the world is going to go through and take a penalty for, we don't have to take the penalty for because our Lord Jesus already took it. ***(2Co.5:21) Him who knew no sin he made [to be] sin on our behalf; that we might become the righteousness of God in him.*** He became cursed for us, He bore the penalty on the Cross. What should we fear? ***(Psa.27:1) The Lord is my light and my salvation; Whom shall I fear? The Lord is the strength of my life; Of whom shall I be afraid?***

(Php.4:6) In nothing be <u>anxious</u> (Some versions say "careful," however the Greek word there, *merimnaó*, specifically means "anxious."); ***but in everything by prayer and supplication with thanksgiving let your requests be made known unto God.*** Since we have such authority with God, such promises from God, what is "anxiety"? It is <u>unbelief</u>, that's what it is. You and I do not believe that the Word of God is true whenever we give in to this temptation. It is sin, we need to look at it as sin, and we need to cast it down just like we would any other kind of sin. ***(Rev.21:8) But for the <u>fearful</u>, and <u>unbelieving</u>, and abominable, and murderers, and fornicators, and sorcerers, and idolaters, and all liars, their part [shall be] in the lake that burneth with fire and brimstone; which is the second death.*** You would never think of doing some of those things that are mentioned there, but would you consider fear and anxiety to be in the same category? Would you consider them to be sin before God? Would you consider unbelief to be sin before the King? If someone is unbelieving, then they are not justified because they are not letting God be true and every man a liar (Romans 3:4). And, if they are not justified, that means their sins are not covered.

We Can Trust God Because He Controls All Things

So God says, "In nothing be anxious," because He is absolutely sovereign. We truly have nothing to worry about since He has everything under control. Let's go back to the beginning of this chapter for a closer look because the Lord showed me, many years ago, a neat revelation here that He hid in the Word just for us. You know, He wants us to stand steadfast and unmovable in Him (Colossians 1:23). He doesn't want us to be moved by what we see or what we hear. You are about to hear of horrendous things in this world. You are about to see horrendous things in this world. He doesn't want us to be moved by those things at all. Just remember, we are the ones to whom God is giving a demonstration. We are the ones He wants to teach. He doesn't want to destroy us; He has good plans for us. Keep that in mind. All these promises concerning you are true, and they are true for <u>you</u>.

(Php.4:1) Wherefore, my brethren beloved and longed for, my joy and crown, so stand fast in the Lord, my beloved. (2) I exhort <u>Euodia</u>, and I exhort <u>Syntyche</u>, to be of the same mind in the Lord. The Lord spoke to me one day when I read this. He spoke to me to go look these names up, and I did. "Euodia" means "to be successful in reaching a goal; to succeed in reaching." "Syntyche" is just the opposite. It means "to meet with an accident." They are opposite names here, with opposite meanings. In other words, sometimes you just walk in the success of the Lord and sometimes you meet with an accident, but the Lord is saying to be of the same mind, no matter which one you are going through. As a matter of fact, He also tells us that we should be content in either case. **(Php.4:11) Not that I speak in respect of want: for I have learned, <u>in whatsoever state I am</u>, <u>therein to be content</u>.** He says that because everything that comes to you, saints, comes to you from the Hand of God (John 3:27). He wants you to trust in Him.

(Php.4:2) I exhort Euodia, and I exhort Syntyche, to be of the same mind in the Lord. (3) Yea, I beseech thee also, true yokefellow, help these women, for they labored with me in the gospel, with Clement also, and the rest of my fellow-work-

ers, whose names are in the book of life. Yes, they do; they labor with all of us in the Gospel, and they labor with us in our own life, and in bearing fruit and so on and so forth. Saints, God wants us to be stable and not moved up and down by our emotions, not moved by every wind of doctrine, not moved by anything that happens in the world. He wants us to be steadfast, standing on His Word like standing on a rock. In one of the first visions we received, I was shown standing on a rock with leg braces on. The interpretation is that God's external power was helping me to stand upon the Rock. I was able to stand only by His grace and power, not by any power of my own.

He said, "these women ... labored with me in the gospel, with Clement also." "Clement" means "merciful." Jesus said, ***(Mat.5:7) Blessed are the merciful: for they shall obtain mercy.*** With those who will have mercy towards others, and be forgiving towards others, God will show Himself the same way. Sometimes we do much harm to ourselves in the way that we relate to others, as in the Parable of the Unforgiving Servant. ***(Mat.18:34) And his lord was wroth, and <u>delivered him to the tormentors</u>, till he should pay all that was due. (35) So shall also my heavenly Father do unto you, if ye forgive not every one his brother from your hearts.*** He turns you over to the tormentors, so we need to be merciful and we need to not be moved by success or failure. ***(Php.4:4) Rejoice in the Lord always: again I will say, Rejoice. (5) Let your forbearance be known unto all men. The Lord is at hand.*** (So much the more today!) ***(6) In nothing be anxious; but in everything by prayer and supplication with thanksgiving let your requests be made known***

unto God. In other words, don't worry about a thing; just lay your request before God. Remember that Jesus said, **(Mar.11:24) ... *All things whatsoever ye pray and ask for, believe that ye received them, and ye shall have them.***

Are we going to be anxious, or are we going to believe? As we've seen, anxiety is totally against faith and it is a sin against God (Revelation 21:8), but if you know that, you know that you can cast it down. You can put up your shield of faith, and quench that fiery dart. You don't have to let the *skorpizo* spirit penetrate you and put you to flight. Many people are not acting on the Word, instead, they are re-acting to what the devil is doing around them. Guess what they are ruled by? If you are not ruled by faith, you are going to be ruled by fear. **(Luk.11:23) *He that is not with me is against me; and he that gathereth not with me scattereth.*** If you want to be moved and ruled by the Lord, then remember anxiety and fear is sin. When anxiety and fear comes to people's hearts immediately after some disaster, this is the devil seeking to bring them into bondage and it must be cast down immediately.

Perfect Peace in the Midst of Trials

(Php.4:7) *And the peace of God, which passeth all understanding, shall guard your hearts and your thoughts in Christ Jesus.* We need the peace of God in the midst of turmoil. **(Isa.26:3) *Thou wilt keep [him] in perfect peace, [whose] mind [is] stayed [on thee]; because he trusteth in thee.*** Oh, glory to God! Keep your mind on what God has said, on what He has taught you, and cast down everything else the devil fires your way. God will keep you in perfect peace while other people are falling apart. They will be going this way while you will be going that way. You know, when you react to the devil, he's herding you in the direction he wants you to go and you're proving that you are one of his pack. If you follow him, you are one of his. You're proving who you follow by how you handle these trials that you are going through, these things that are really not "accidents," because nothing can come into your life by accident. They are trials from the Lord that He has absolute control over, otherwise, how could He say "in nothing be anxious"? And how could He say that He works all things together for your good (Romans 8:28)? He can say that because He is in absolute control and you can trust Him. You can rest in His promises, therefore, don't let anxiety or fear affect you. Cast them down.

(Php.4:8) Finally, brethren, whatsoever things are _true_ (Who is the Truth? Jesus Christ, the Word of God, is Truth, and He promises to keep you in perfect peace if your mind is stayed on Him {Isaiah 26;3}.)**, whatsoever things are honorable, whatsoever things are just, whatsoever things are pure, whatsoever things are lovely, whatsoever things are of _good report_...** We want to believe and remember the "good report." It doesn't make any difference what happens in the world around us. We have to hold fast to the good report. When the Israelites were moved by fear and anxiety, they cried out to God, claiming He had brought them to that wilderness to die (Numbers 21:5), which was so foolish, but you think that way when you are under the dominion of fear and anxiety. The Lord has not brought us anywhere to fail, but to teach us to be sons of God, if we will only keep our mind upon Him, upon the Word of God, upon the good report. Remember, the Israelites listened to the bad report from the spies who did not have any faith in God (Numbers 13:31-33). Their faith was in the bad report. They believed that they could <u>not</u> conquer that land or those giants, which in type represented the old man of the flesh (Numbers 14:2-4). ***(Php.4:8) Finally, brethren, whatsoever things are true, whatsoever things are honorable, whatsoever things are just, whatsoever things are pure, whatsoever things are lovely, whatsoever things are of good report; <u>if there be any virtue</u>, <u>and if there be any praise</u>, <u>think on these things</u>.*** Refuse to think on the things that are going to destroy you, or cause you to be manipulated, or cause you to be herded before the demons of the devil so that you partake of their curse.

(Php.4:9) The things which ye both learned and received and heard and saw in me, these things do: and the God of peace shall be with you. Paul was telling them, ***(1Co.11:1) Be ye imitators of me, even as I also am of Christ.*** Or, in other words, "Follow me, as I follow the Lord." Even today, folks, when you see people who are following the Lord and being a good example, pay attention to their witness and their testimony. There are many people out there speaking only from their theology, but with no experience whatsoever. They haven't walked with God by faith and they're leading God's people into Babylon. "The things which ye both learned and received and heard and <u>saw</u> in me, these things do: and the God of peace shall be with you." This is what we want, folks. We want to walk in the peace of God. ***(Isa.26:3) Thou wilt keep [him] in perfect peace, [whose] mind***

[is] stayed [on thee]; because he trusteth in thee.

If we permit the devil to penetrate our defense, which is faith in the Word of God, then the fiery dart of the "stinger" will come through. If you are not ***(Eph.6:16) ... taking up the shield of faith, wherewith ye shall be able to quench all the fiery darts of the evil [one]***, then you'll be overcome by emotions. You'll do what the world does and so you'll fall under the judgment of the world. As we've seen, this is exactly what the Israelites did in the wilderness, when they fell under the judgment of the world and under the curse of Deuteronomy 28. Except for Joshua and Caleb, they died in the wilderness instead of overcoming and entering into the Promised Land. "But I am persuaded of better things of you," Paul said. "I am persuaded that the Lord is able to keep you and to bring you through these troubling times in boldness and in courage" (Hebrews 6:9-12,18-19). Make sure, saints, that there is nothing in your heart that will hinder, nothing in your heart that will separate you from that boldness that God gives to those who are <u>obedient</u>, because ***(1Jn.3:21) Beloved, if our heart condemn us not, we have boldness toward God...*** And that boldness will bring you peace. ***(Php.4:9) The things which ye both learned and received and heard and saw in me, these things do: and the God of peace shall be with you.***

There is one passage in the Bible where Jesus spoke about anxiety; it's in Matthew chapter 6 and He mentioned it six times. He did not do that anywhere else. We're going to look at that because it's where an awful lot of Christians struggle. We are heading toward a wilderness trial, folks, and one thing we find in a wilderness trial is that the Lord suffers His people to see lack. He suffers them to be tried in order to see what they will do. In all the places where the Lord led His people Israel in the wilderness, it was from one trial to the next. They were always seeing lack ahead of them, lack of water, lack of food, lack of protection from enemies, and so on and so forth. Of course, they had many opportunities to be penetrated by fear and anxiety. They had many opportunities to run in the opposite direction, to cry out in unbelief, and even to accuse God of things that He had no mind to do. ***(Num.14:2) And all the children of Israel murmured against Moses and against Aaron: and the whole congregation said unto them, Would that we had died in the land of Egypt! or would that we had died in this wilderness! (3) And wherefore doth the Lord bring us unto this land, to fall by the sword? ...*** You know, they finally convinced Him and it was exactly what they needed. It was their own fault, too, because God told Moses, ***(Num.14:28) Say unto them, As I live, saith the Lord, <u>surely as ye have spoken in mine ears, so will I do to you: (29) your dead bodies shall fall in this wilderness</u>; and all that were numbered of you, according to your whole number, from twenty years old and upward, that have murmured against me, (30) surely ye shall not come into the land, concerning which I sware that I would make you dwell therein, save Caleb the son of Jephunneh, and Joshua the son of Nun.*** That's what they had faith for and so He gave it to them, because ***(Mat.9:29) ... According to your faith be it done unto you.*** Anxiety and fear is faith; it is just negative faith, faith in the curse and in the devil, and God will let you have the curse if you believe in it.

I know there are some of you who don't believe there is anything to come but peace and prosperity to God's people because of how special they are. Folks, you are missing history. Please read the Bible again because God's people went through fiery trials. They were hated of the nations, and Jesus said it's going to be the same for us. ***(Mat.24:9) Then shall they deliver you up unto tribulation, and shall kill you: and <u>ye shall be hated of all the nations for my name's sake</u>. (10) And then shall many stumble, and shall deliver up one another, and shall hate one another. (11) And many false prophets shall arise, and shall lead many astray. (12) And because iniquity shall be multiplied, the love of the many shall wax cold. (13) But he that endureth to the end, the same shall be saved.*** Most of us have never gone through any of that, but none of us have gone through the hatred of the whole world against Christianity. The Lord is raising-up a very big enemy against His small group of elect, exactly the way it was with Israel. And He's going to take a lot of worldly provision away from His people in the days to come, so that their provision will come from heaven. The Lord is going to provide for His people. He's going to show Himself strong on behalf of them that have put their faith and trust in Him.

Let Your Eye Be Single

Now I would like to read what Jesus had to say concerning His provision for you in the times to come. Notice that in this passage where Jesus mentions the word "anxious" six times, it is always the same Greek word *merimnaó*, which we just read in Philippians. ***(Php.4:6) In***

nothing be <u>anxious</u>; but in everything by prayer and supplication with thanksgiving let your requests be made known unto God. Well, here in Matthew we see He is teaching the people, and it seems their anxiety was always about their provision, the things that they needed in order to be able to live in the wilderness. He tells them, ***(Mat.6:19) Lay not up for yourselves treasures upon the earth, where moth and rust consume, and where thieves break through and steal: (20) but lay up for yourselves treasures in heaven, where neither moth nor rust doth consume, and where thieves do not break through nor steal*** (Many of God's people have their confidence in what <u>they</u> can store-up, not in what God promised He would do.)***: (21) for where thy treasure is, there will thy heart be also.*** Of course, your treasure is something that you stored up as a provision for your future, so that is where your heart, your trust, will be. ***(22) The lamp of the body is the eye: if therefore thine eye be single, thy whole body shall be full of light.*** In other words, an "eye" that is "single" is not an eye that is set upon its own provisions; it's not set upon things that it has stored-up to save self in the days to come. ***(23) But if thine eye be evil, thy whole body shall be full of darkness. If therefore, the light that is in thee be darkness, how great is the darkness!*** An "eye" that is "dark" is an eye that has its confidence in the things of this world, and I am going to prove that to you as we read on. ***(24) No man can serve two masters; for either he will hate the one, and love the other; or else he will hold to one, and despise the other. Ye cannot serve God and mammon.*** Those "two masters" He's talking about are God and mammon. *Mamónas* is the Aramaic word for "riches, money, possessions, property," and it comes from an Old Testament Hebrew word *matmon*, which means "hidden treasures," while *mammōnás* means "the treasure a person trusts (has confidence) in."

So "mammon" here represents trusting in worldly treasures that are stored-up or hidden, trusting in the things of the world to provide salvation. As you know, when the Israelites came out of Egypt, God permitted them to have something they trusted in, gold and silver, that was given into their hands by the Egyptians, by the world (Exodus 3:22). And, again, they made an idol out of this, meaning they trusted in it. God wanted them to be tried in this way because He was the one that permitted them to go out there with this gold. However, His plan was to try them to see if they would be faithful, and they weren't. They made an idol out of that gold (Exodus 32:4), the thing that they had stored-up to preserve them through their wilderness trials. God wanted to meet their needs out of heaven; that was His plan from the beginning but first He had to get the gold out of the way. **(Exo.32:20) And he** (That is Moses.) **took the calf which they had made, and burnt it with fire, and ground it to powder, and strewed it upon the water, and <u>made the children of Israel drink of it</u>.** In other words, "I hope you remember this lesson."

People who are trusting in the things that they are storing-up for the times to come, are doing it because they do not believe the Word of God. They do not believe that **(Php.4:19) ... my God shall supply every need of yours according to his riches in glory in Christ Jesus.** They are anxious, troubled, and fearful. Their trust and confidence is in mammon. They have the eye that is evil. Their eye is not single. Let's read on and see if Jesus confirms this. **(Mat.6:25) Therefore I say unto you, be not <u>anxious</u>** (There is the first one of six mentions, and again, it's the same word, *merimnaó,* that we read in Philippians 4:6.) ***for your life, what ye shall eat, or what ye shall drink; nor yet for your body, what ye shall put on.*** We don't have to worry about these things. We don't have to worry about preparing in our own strength to preserve ourselves through the days to come. Many people claim they have received words from the "Lord" about preparing for themselves. I tell you, folks, we are coming to a time when God wants to prove His power to save you by signs and wonders and miracles, not by your own worldly methods. God's provision came out of heaven to God's people in the wilderness. He did not want them to be anxious; He did not want them to be fearful. He wanted them to trust in His provision alone, so He ran them out of everything that they provided for themselves when they came out of Egypt and then He provided for them. They received water out of the rock (Numbers 20:11) and manna out of heaven (Exodus 16:4) and quail out of the sky (Exodus 16:12). We are coming to the exact same repetition of history today, except this time it is for the Church. Once again God is going to provide for those who believe.

(Mat.6:25) Therefore I say unto you, be not anxious for your life, what ye shall eat, or what ye shall drink; nor yet for your body, what ye shall put on. Is not the life more than the food, and the body than the raiment? (26) Behold the birds of the heaven, that they sow not, neither do they reap, nor gather into barns; and your heavenly Father feedeth them. Have you ever thought that if you could not provide for yourself or if the economy went down, which it will, and you could not work, that God would provide for you? Well, I guarantee you He will provide if you walk by faith, but where He says "they sow not," is God teaching that you don't need to work for a living? Obviously not, because Paul told us, **(2Th.3:10) For even when we were with you, this we commanded you, <u>If any will not work</u>, <u>neither let him eat</u>. (11) For we hear of some that walk among you disorderly, that work not at all, but are busybodies. (12) Now them that are such we command and exhort in the Lord Jesus Christ, that with quietness they work, and eat their own bread.** I'll tell you what I believe is going to happen. I believe there is going to be a great exchange in these days, God's people are finally going to wake up and take the Great Commission seriously. **(Mat.28:19) Go ye therefore, and make disciples of all the nations, baptizing them into the name of the Father and of the Son and of the Holy Spirit.** Jesus said **(Luk.11:23) ... he that gathereth not with me, scattereth.** He wants us gathering and He raises up disciples to do His work of the Great Commission and if you are not working for the world, you can work for Him. Even the birds and the flowers work for Him, but they don't toil in the world and God still feeds the birds and clothes the flowers.

(Mat.6:26) Behold the birds of the heaven, that they sow not, neither do they reap, <u>nor gather into barns</u> (They're not storing up their treasures, their food, for the days to come.)**; and your heavenly Father feedeth them. Are not ye of much more value than they? (27) And which of you by being <u>anxious</u>**

(There's the second mention.) ***can add one cubit unto the measure of his life?*** We know that anxiety does nothing but destroy you, physically, mentally, emotionally. It brings sickness because it tears down your immunity. Faith can beat anything, but anxiety can do nothing except bring you more harm. ***(Mat.6:28) And why are ye <u>anxious</u>*** (There's the third mention.) ***concerning raiment? Consider the lilies of the field, how they grow; they toil not, neither do they spin: (29) yet I say unto you, that even Solomon in all his glory was not arrayed like one of these.*** (Wow!) ***(30) But if God doth so clothe the grass of the field, which today is, and tomorrow is cast into the oven, [shall he] not much more [clothe] you, O ye of little faith?*** The Lord is going to take care of you; don't worry about a thing. Some of you are going to lose your jobs, which you so prize, and maybe your high standard of living. However, you are going to exchange your attitude towards the world and the things of the world, for one that is like those of the disciples in Jesus' day. Folks, Christians were plundered in Jesus' day. When those Jews became Christians, they were plundered. Nobody would do business with them. Basically, they were in a wilderness, yet the Lord provided for them because they put their trust in Him.

(Mat.6:31) Be not therefore <u>anxious</u> (There's the fourth mention.)***, saying, what shall we eat? or, What shall we drink? or, Wherewithal shall we be clothed?*** Why did He keep mentioning the same thing? It's because He knew the carnal nature and He knew the trials that were coming for the Jewish Christians in these days. When Jesus spoke this back then, they were in the beginning of the first 3-1/2 years of their tribulation. He knew what they were going through, and He knew what we are going to go through in our day, which is the same thing, folks. There is a great economic collapse coming, but God has made this promise that He is going to provide for His people. Don't give in to any anxiety and fear. Know that God has said He is your Jehovah-Jireh. **(Gen.22:14) And Abraham called the name of that place Jehovah-jireh: as it is said to this day, In the mount of the Lord it shall be provided.** He is going to provide for you in everything. He wants to show you His Glory. He wants to show you His Power.

(Mat.6:31) Be not therefore anxious, saying, What shall we eat? or, What shall we drink? or, Wherewithal shall we be clothed? (32) For after all these things do the Gentiles (These were the unsaved heathen at that time.) **seek; for your heavenly Father knoweth that ye have need of all these things.** Yes, He already knows this. You don't have to worry, you don't have to beg, and you don't have to spend hours and hours on your knees. All you have to do is, **(Php.4:6) In nothing be anxious; but in everything by prayer and supplication with thanksgiving let your requests be made known unto God.** You are not going to be heard for your "much speaking" (Matthew 6:7). Don't be fearful or anxious because of what you see, or because it appears as if you're coming to the end of your own provision. God is bringing you there because you need to be at the end of your own provision before you can receive God's provision. He wants to show you a miracle; He wants to show you many miracles.

(Mat.6:33) But seek ye first his kingdom, and his righteousness; and all these things shall be

added unto you. God is going to make sure that you are provided for as you seek first His Kingdom, as you seek to build His Kingdom both in your life and in the lives of the people around you. Seek first His Kingdom and He is going to make sure that you are going to have everything that you need. Of course, if you are seeking His Kingdom, you are not going to have a love of the world. ***(1Jn.2:15) Love not the world, neither the things that are in the world. If any man love the world, the love of the Father is not in him.*** The love of the world is sin; the love of the Father is not. I would say the overwhelming number of Christians have a problem with a love of the world, and they are even taught to love the world in their prosperity-minded churches. They have to have the things of the world, but the Bible doesn't call that "prosperity." ***(3Jn.1:2) Beloved, I pray that in all things thou mayest prosper*** (The Greek word there is *euodoó* meaning "to have a successful journey." It's the same root for the name "Euodia" that means "successful in reaching a goal" in Philippians 4:2.) ***and be in health, even as thy soul prospereth.*** That's *euodoó* again so it's not talking about having material riches.

(Mat.6:34) Be not therefore anxious for the morrow: for the morrow will be anxious for itself. (These are the fifth and sixth mentions of "anxious" by Jesus. He said not to be anxious about our provisions, about our needs being met, because God would take care of it.) ***Sufficient unto the day is the evil thereof.*** Jesus is commanding us, "Don't worry about tomorrow. The Lord is going to take care of it for you. You don't have to be fearful." He reminds us, ***(Luk.12:32) Fear not, little flock; for it is your Father's good pleasure to***

give you the kingdom. Oh, glory to God! It certainly is. Now I would like to show you what <u>He</u> says is important. ***(Luk.10:38) Now as they went on their way, he entered into a certain village: and a certain woman named Martha received him into her house. (39) And she had a sister called Mary, who also sat at the Lord's feet, and heard his word. (40) But Martha was cumbered about much serving; and she came up to him, and said, Lord, dost thou not care that my sister did leave me to serve alone? bid her therefore that she help me. (41) But the Lord answered and said unto her, "Martha, Martha, thou art anxious and troubled about many things: (42) but one thing is needful: for Mary hath chosen the good part, which shall not be taken away from her.*** Folks, don't be worried and anxious about how to serve God or what to do in this world. There is just one thing that is important: we need to sit at His feet and listen to Him.

CHAPTER EIGHT

Anxiety and Fear, Part 2

Casting Down Fear

As we're learning, there are some great shakings, some great judgments, coming across the world in these days, and the devil always uses things that we see and things that we hear to try to bring fear upon God's people. Whenever something happens, immediately the devil or his demons pounce and you feel the spirit of fear come over you like a blanket. Well, we're obviously meant to make war against that, so don't accept any fear as if it's just a personal weakness and allow it to stay. Remember, we spoke about the *skorpizo* spirits, whose job it is "to penetrate and put to flight." They cause a person to be fearful or anxious. They cause a person to flee from the devil and, of course, then they're no threat against his kingdom.

Fear is one of the devil's "big guns," but the Bible says, **(2Ti.1:7) For <u>God gave us not a spirit of fearfulness</u>; but of power and love and <u>discipline</u>.** The word there translated "discipline" comes from the Greek *sóphronizó* and literally means "sober-mindedness; control." If you're not walking in willful disobedience when a spirit of fear comes upon you, you know that it's not from God. It's from the devil and you shouldn't receive it or give-in to it or think about it, because if you do, it's going to conquer you. It comes for the purpose of penetrating your armor (Ephesians 6:10-17) and putting you to flight. We know the only fear that we should have is the fear of the Lord, which is the beginning of wisdom (Psalm 111:10;

Proverbs 1:7,9:10; etc.) If we fear the Lord, we will depart from unrighteousness, as the Bible says (2 Timothy 2:19). Any other fear, such as the fear of man, brings a snare. God didn't give us a spirit of fear, but if you're walking in willful disobedience, you're proving that you don't fear the Lord. If you don't fear the Lord, you will have fear of the devil, which is foolishness because it is giving faith to the devil. Fear is faith, but it's negative faith; it's faith in the curse, faith in the devil, faith in failure. It's as our Lord Jesus told us, **(Mat.9:29) ... *According to your faith be it done unto you.*** And that's one reason why Job said, **(Job.3:25) *For the thing which I fear cometh upon me, And that which I am afraid of cometh unto me.*** It's important for us to understand that our fears come to pass, just like our faiths do. They're opposite reactions, but both of them are faith. Saints, we are supposed to be overcomers.

(Rev.21:7) *He that overcometh* shall inherit these things... Of course, the Lord is implying that if you don't overcome, you're not going to inherit the new heaven and new earth and all the great things that God has provided for His people (Revelation 21:1-4). There are those who don't think we have anything to overcome. They think that Jesus overcame it all, which is true, but Jesus overcame so that we could overcome. We learn to abide in Him and see those works manifest. The Bible says, **(Jas.2:17) *Even so faith, if it have not works, is dead in itself.*** Overcomers are sons of God and they will inherit the Kingdom.

(Rev.21:7) *He that overcometh shall inherit these things; and I will be his God, and he shall be my son.* Now the next verse puts "fear" and "unbelief" together, because if you are fearful, then you are unbelieving, and if you are unbelieving, then you will be fearful.

Notice "He that overcometh," is not an overcomer unless these things are overcome. ***(Rev.21:8) But for the fearful, and unbelieving, and abominable, and murderers, and fornicators, and sorcerers, and idolaters, and all liars, their part [shall be] in the lake that burneth with fire and brimstone; which is the second death.*** "Fearful" and "unbelieving" are grouped right in there with these really abominable sins. So fear is more than a weakness, it's a sin, and it's unbelief. The Bible calls it "an evil heart of unbelief." ***(Heb.3:12) Take heed, brethren, lest haply there shall be in any one of you <u>an evil heart of unbelief</u>, in falling away from the living God.*** Fear is something we need to make war against whenever we feel its presence, whenever we have fearful thoughts. Fear can manifest in even worse ways but most of all, it causes us to run from the devil and give up the fight. It causes us to lose ground.

Just as the fearful and the unbelieving are among the wicked, obviously, there's a part of every one of us that is wicked, and it's that old man that we want to overcome. ***(Gal.5:17) For the flesh lusteth against the Spirit, and the Spirit against the flesh; for these are contrary the one to the other; that ye may not do the things that ye would.*** There's a war going on in every one of us, yet we can overcome through faith in the victory that Jesus had at the Cross. ***(1Co.15:22) For as in Adam all die, so also in Christ shall all be made alive.*** When Christ was resurrected, we were resurrected, too. We received His resurrection life. When He overcame, we also overcame. ***(Gal.2:20) I have been crucified with Christ; and it is no longer I that live, but Christ living in me: and that [life] which I now live in the***

flesh I live in faith, [the faith] which is in the Son of God, who loved me, and gave himself up for me. We were crucified with Christ and the old man was put to death with Christ, but we need to hold on to our faith to see it <u>manifested</u> in the physical realm. The gift that has been given to us, we can overcome to receive.

There's an awesome revelation I want to share with you where God calls the fearful "wicked," which is another confirmation that we need to fight against this spirit. ***(Job.15:20) The wicked man travaileth with pain all his days, Even the number of years that are laid up for the oppressor. (21) A sound of <u>terrors</u> is in his ears; In prosperity the destroyer shall come upon him.*** Isn't that amazing? Some of the words we hear most these days are "terror" and "terrorist" and "terrorism"! You know, I believe we are coming to the end of the "seven years of plenty" that was prophesied by Joseph and we're coming to the beginning of the "seven years of famine" (Genesis 41). We can look around us and see that this is coming upon the prosperous.

The Wicked Don't Believe

(Job.15:22) He believeth not that he shall return out of darkness... The wicked are in terror and they don't believe that they will return out of darkness, but that's not believing the Gospel. That's not believing the Good News. ***(Col.1:12) Giving thanks unto the Father, who made us meet to be partakers of the inheritance of the saints in light; (13) <u>who delivered us out of the power of darkness</u>, <u>and translated us into the kingdom of the Son of his love</u>; (14) in***

whom we have our redemption, the forgiveness of our sins. That's the Good News we are to believe, but the wicked don't believe and so they live in terror. ***(Job.15:22) He believeth not that he shall return out of darkness, And he is waited for of the sword. (23) He wandereth abroad for bread, [saying], Where is it? He knoweth that the day of darkness is ready at his hand. (24) Distress and anguish make him afraid; They prevail against him, as a king ready to the battle.*** The devil conquers and rules the wicked by fear. If you are ruled by fear, if you act according to your fear, then you're submitting to the devil's kingdom instead of God, because He hasn't given us a spirit of fearfulness. If you're ruled by fear, you're not ruled by God <u>and</u> you're in idolatry because you're having faith in the devil.

(Job.15:25) Because he hath stretched out his hand against God, And behaveth himself proudly against the Almighty. Fear is part of the judgment that comes upon the wicked because they're acting against God. God turns over to the devil those who walk in sin. This is true even of the Kingdom people. Jesus said, ***(Mat.18:34) And his lord was wroth, and delivered him to the tormentors, till he should pay all that was due.*** He had them turned over to the tormentors, but the wicked of the world are already turned over to the tormentors. They live in torment, but the righteous are believing God and they're coming out of the kingdom of darkness. The wicked do not believe God, so they live under the tormentors, which include fear and anxiety. Since they have stretched out their hand against God, He has delivered them over to this fear. We're told, ***(1Jn.3:21) Beloved, if our heart condemn us not, we have boldness toward God;***

(22) and whatsoever we ask we receive of him, because we keep his commandments and do the things that are pleasing in his sight. If we have a clear conscience, we have boldness and not fear. When God does allow fear to come upon a person who has a clear conscience, God is allowing it to come as a trial unto them, and their boldness is the very thing that will vanquish it.

(Pro.28:1) The <u>wicked</u> flee when no man pursueth; But the righteous are bold as a lion. Fear is natural and normal to the wicked. Who are the "wicked"? The wicked are those who sin. It doesn't matter whether you're a Christian or not, if you're walking in willful sin, you're wicked. You don't have boldness toward God and His benefits in that case because your conscience condemns you. You want a defense against fear in the days to come, because you're going to see and hear things that are fearful, and that's when the devil pounces upon you. That's when he tries to overcome you so that you're full of fear and are just running from him. Jesus told us, **(Mat.12:30) He that is not with me is against me, and he that gathereth not with me scattereth.** If we're not plundering the devil's kingdom, we <u>are</u> going to be running from him. Without a clear conscience, we have guilt. Demons use this to condemn you so that you have no faith toward God and His Word. When you don't know the Gospel, when you don't know that your failures and ignorances are covered by the Blood (James 4:17), you can have false guilt, which Satan can use to deliver you over to fear.

As a matter of fact, that's what happened to Adam. Adam had only one commandment to obey, **(Gen.2:17) ... of the tree of the knowledge of good and evil, thou shalt not eat of it: for in the day that thou**

eatest thereof thou shalt surely die. But Adam broke that commandment. ***(Gen.3:7) And the eyes of them both were opened, and they knew that they were naked...*** "Nakedness" here is a representation of the guilt of sin. They didn't know they were naked until they partook of the fruit "of the tree of the knowledge of good and evil." Now they were made sinners because now they knew they had broken God's law, and so guilt is the first thing they received. ***(Gen.3:7) And the eyes of them both were opened, and they knew that they were naked; and they sewed fig-leaves together, and made themselves aprons.*** Obviously, they were attempting to cover their guilt. Men do try to cover their guilt in various ways through self-works.

As we know, ***(Gen.3:21) And the Lord God made for Adam and for his wife <u>coats of skins</u>, and clothed them.*** God slew animals, and without the shedding of blood, there is no covering for our sins (Hebrews 9:22). He didn't accept their self-works to alleviate their guilt. ***(Gen.3:8) And they heard the voice of the Lord God walking in the garden in the cool of the day: <u>and the man and his wife hid themselves from the presence of the Lord God</u> amongst the trees of the garden.*** Many people, including Christians, are hiding themselves because of their guilt. They don't want to face God and they don't like to read the Word because it condemns them. They don't know the great Sacrifice that the Lord has made for them to be given grace to overcome. Guilt makes them feel bad when they face themselves, when they read the Word, and so forth. ***(Gen.3:9) And the Lord God called unto the man, and said unto him, Where art thou? (10) And he said, I heard thy*** *voice in the garden, and I was afraid, because I was naked; and I hid myself.* Guilt brings fear. If you don't want to be overcome by fear, you need to confess your sins because, *(1Jn.1:9) If we confess our sins, he is faithful and righteous to forgive us our sins, and to cleanse us from all unrighteousness.* We need to repent, confess our sins, and have faith that Jesus has given us authority over this old flesh.

The real Good News is that the Lord wants to live the Christian life in us; He wants to be *(Col.1:27) ... Christ in you, the hope of glory.* Many people are living under the bondage of guilt and there is no reason to be doing that when the real Good News is that He's already set us free. *(Rom.8:2) For the law of the Spirit of life in Christ Jesus made me free from the law of sin and of death.* If you have guilt, the devil can use that to conquer you with fear because then you don't have boldness towards God. You know, folks, sometimes we get so far down that we're willing to look up, and sometimes the Lord lets the devil take advantage of us until we're willing to get our eyes on Him and to have faith in what He's accomplished at the Cross. Faith that brings obedience gives us victory over fear. *(Lev.26:13) I am the Lord your God, who brought you forth out of the land of Egypt...* As Christians, we, too, have been delivered out of the "land of Egypt." Spiritually speaking, "Egypt" represents the world, and we've been delivered from bondage to the world, delivered from bondage to the old man, who is the "Egyptian." *(Lev.26:13) I am the Lord your God, who brought you forth out of the land of Egypt, that ye should not be their bondmen; and I have broken the bars of your yoke, and made you go*

upright. This is basically the Gospel, isn't it? You've <u>been</u> delivered: He made you free from sin. You're no longer in bondage to the old man.

(Lev.26:14) But if ye will not hearken unto me, and will not do all these commandments (Notice how many times He says the same thing over and over here.)*; (15) and if ye shall reject my statutes, and if your soul abhor mine ordinances, so that ye will not do all my commandments* (He's making sure that we get the point.)*, but break my covenant; (16) I also will do this unto you:* <u>*I will appoint terror over you*</u> (God delivers people who are rebellious against His Word over to fear.)*, even consumption and fever, that shall consume the eyes, and make the soul to pine away; and ye shall sow your seed in vain, for your enemies shall eat it.* Yes, many people are constantly plundered by the devil. They're delivered over to fear because they're rebellious against His Word. They have no boldness to come against the devil and they don't understand why they're being devoured by the devourer (Malachi 3:11). *(Lev.26:17) And I will set my face against you, and ye shall be smitten before your enemies: they that hate you shall rule over you; and <u>ye shall flee when none pursueth you</u>.* This is exactly what we read earlier: *(Pro.28:1) The wicked flee when no man pursueth; But the righteous are bold as a lion.* So we see that God appoints terror over rebellious people, whether they are God's rebellious people or the people of the world. Terror in these days, I believe, is something that God has loosed through the devil to motivate people to run to Him, to run to repentance and faith and boldness, so that we may be delivered of these things.

Fear gives control to the devil, who will bring us right back into bondage in Egypt.

We've Been Divided and Scattered

(Deu.28:64) And the Lord will scatter thee among all peoples, from the one end of the earth even unto the other end of the earth... A lot of people don't realize that everything that happened to Israel in the Old Testament, happens to the Church in a spiritual way. The Church was said by Peter to be just <u>one</u> holy nation (1 Peter 2:9), and Paul said that we were grafted into the olive tree called "<u>all</u> Israel" (Romans 11:17-26). We are <u>one</u> people, but we've been divided and scattered. The Bible talks about the shepherds that scatter the flock (Jeremiah 10:21; Ezekiel 34:6; Matthew 26:31; etc.) We've been divided and scattered and brought into bondage to the nations of the world. Now God is calling us out of those nations to our one Holy Nation, which is spiritual Israel (2 Corinthians 6:17; Revelation 18:4). We've been called out from among them, but when we rebel against God, He brings us under the spirit of fear and we go back into bondage. **(Deu.28:64) And the Lord will scatter thee among all peoples, from the one end of the earth even unto the other end of the earth; and there thou shalt serve other <u>gods</u>, which thou hast not known, thou nor thy fathers, even wood and stone.** The Hebrew word "gods" there is also translated as "mighty ones." If you want to know who are the church's mighty ones, just ask, "What kind of gods is the church serving?" Much of what we call the "church," by their own actions, prove that they have trust in their government, trust in their military, trust in their doctors, trust in their bank accounts, trust in their insurance policies, and on and on. These are the "mighty ones" that the church is trusting in because they're in bondage to the nations of the world, instead of being part of the nation of spiritual Israel, but the Lord has called us out. He has called us out of Egypt that we might be His holy nation.

(Deu.28:65) And among these nations shalt thou find no ease, and there shall be no rest for the sole of thy foot: but the Lord will give thee there a <u>trembling heart</u> (When you're living in the world, God says over and over that He's going to give you fear, and of course, we should be afraid to live in the world because there's no eternal life there. There's nothing but the curse.)**, and failing of eyes, and pining of soul; (66) and thy life shall hang in doubt before thee; and thou shalt fear night and day** (Wow! It's obvious this is coming to pass in these days.)**, and shalt have no assurance of thy life.** There's nothing except fear, just fear! **(67) In the morning thou shalt say, Would it were even! and at even thou shalt say, Would it were morning! for the fear of thy heart which thou shalt fear, and for the sight of thine eyes which thou shalt see. (68) And the Lord will bring thee into Egypt <u>again</u>...** Well, let's look at what brought God's people into Egypt the first time. Jacob's twelve sons were the patriarchs, however, they were not obedient to their father, and when Joseph brought the report of them to Jacob, they were offended. **(Gen.37:26) And Judah said unto his brethren, What profit is it if we slay our brother and conceal his blood? (27) Come, and let us sell him to the Ishmaelites, and let not our hand be upon him; for he is our brother, our flesh.**

And his brethren hearkened unto him. (28) And there passed by Midianites, merchantmen; and they drew and lifted up Joseph out of the pit, and sold Joseph to the Ishmaelites for twenty pieces of silver. And they brought Joseph into Egypt. They persecuted the righteous, they persecuted Joseph, and God sent them into 400 years of bondage in Egypt.

(Deu.28:68) ***And the Lord will bring thee into Egypt again*** *with ships, by the way whereof I said unto thee, Thou shalt see it no more again* (God commands that we never go back into Egypt, never go back into bondage to the old man. That's what this is talking about.)*: and there ye shall sell yourselves unto your enemies for bondmen and for bondwomen, and no man shall buy you.* So the Lord gives fear and men go back into bondage to the old man. You know, people do strange things when they fear. One thing they do is that they take control of themselves, instead of trusting in God. Who is "self"? "Self" is the "old man," meaning that you're going back into bondage and the old man is ruling once again. The "Egyptian," who once ruled over the "Israelite" is now ruling over him again because of fear, one of the devil's big guns. When a person is in fear, even a Christian can be brought to killing their fellow man. They have a fear of death so they will run to the arm of the flesh and do what is totally contrary to the Word of God.

We've seen the Word tells us to rest in God, trust in Him, believe that He has already provided whatever the deliverance is that you need because fear causes people to go back into bondage. Fear causes them to have no strength before the enemy. It causes them to run from their enemies, but God delivered us from this and we're not in bondage anymore if we <u>believe</u> the Gospel. We need to believe in order to come out of darkness, as we just read (Job 15:22; Colossians 1:13), but when you have fear, you don't believe that you can come out of darkness, you don't believe the Gospel. When you have fear, you believe the devil and you believe the curse, you don't believe that God has separated you unto Himself to protect, heal, deliver, and provide for you, contrary to the rest of the whole world. What is it that you fear that is <u>not</u> covered by the promises of these things? You need to know that the devil is going to attempt, in these days, to make war on the people of God through the things that they see and the things that they hear in order to bring them into bondage. Our greatest strength, folks, is going to be walking by faith in obedience, because the devil cannot get a foothold if we do that.

The Lord says, **(Pro.1:22) How long, ye simple ones, will ye love <u>simplicity</u>?** (The Hebrew word there for "simplicity" means "lack of knowledge." He's talking about being "simple" in the knowledge of God, in the knowledge of the Word.) **And scoffers delight them in scoffing, <u>And fools hate knowledge</u>?** This is the "simplicity" part, that they hate knowledge. **(23) Turn you at my reproof: Behold, I will pour out <u>my spirit</u> upon you; I will make known <u>my words</u> unto you.** The two things that we desperately need are to have the Word of God sown in our heart, which brings forth the fruit of Christ, and the power of God's Spirit. He's offering us tremendous gifts here, and yet, sometimes, we are not interested, but you can wait until it's too late. **(Pro.1:24) Because I have called, and ye have refused; I have stretched out my hand, and no man hath regarded; (25) But ye have set at nought all my counsel, And would** *none of my reproof: (26) I also will laugh in [the day of] your calamity; I will mock <u>when</u> your fear cometh* (Notice He didn't say, "<u>if</u> your fear cometh," He said, "<u>when</u> your fear cometh." If you continue to reject, beyond the time of God's patience, His Word and His Spirit, He says this fear will come upon you.)*; (27) When your fear cometh as a storm* (Folks, we're going to see that in days to come. Multitudes of people of the earth are going to be swayed this way and that way because of fear and be moved to do terrible things because of fear.)*, And your calamity cometh on as a whirlwind; When distress and anguish come upon you. (28) Then will they call upon me, but I will not answer; They will seek me diligently, but they shall not find me: (29) For that they hated knowledge, And did not choose the fear of the Lord.* Now, obviously, if you have the fear of the Lord, you can't have the fear of the devil. The Bible says, *(Pro.16:6) ... by the fear of the Lord men depart from evil.* You cannot have both at the same time. If you fear the Lord, that's a good fear, because if we fear the Lord, we will serve Him. If we fear the devil, we can't serve the Lord because we're too busy either serving the devil or running from the devil, and that's his plan.

(Pro.1:29) For that they hated knowledge, And did not choose the fear of the Lord, (30) They would none of my counsel, They despised all my reproof. (31) Therefore shall they eat of the fruit of their own way, And be filled with their own devices. (32) For the backsliding of the simple shall slay them (Notice that it's not some man who slays him; it's his own backsliding that slays him.)*, And the careless ease of fools shall destroy them. (33) But who-*

so hearkeneth unto me shall dwell securely (If we are seeking to be obedient to the Lord, putting our faith in Him, trusting in His grace, He empowers us, in turn, to be obedient, and that's a place of security.)***, And shall be quiet without fear of evil.*** The Lord promises this to all those who are obedient because of their faith. Obedience is the fruit of faith. Faith without works is dead (James 2:26) but, of course, these are not man's works; these are God's works through us. Those who are obedient, those who have received grace through their faith to be obedient, will be without fear. The rest will go under the bondage of a spirit of fear.

Be a Son of God, Not a Servant

As a matter of fact, Romans says something very similar to that. ***(Rom.8:12) So then, brethren, we are debtors, not to the flesh, to live after the flesh: (13) for if ye live after the flesh, ye must die; but if by the Spirit ye put to death the deeds of the body, ye shall live. (14) For as many as are led by the Spirit of God, these are sons of God. (15) For ye received not the spirit of bondage again unto fear; but ye received the spirit of adoption, whereby we cry, Abba, Father.*** Jewish scholars say that no servant would dare call "Abba, Father" to the head of a household. This is somebody who has a relationship to the Father, somebody who has the relationship of a child to the father. "As many as are led by the Spirit of God ... are ... sons of God," and that's who this is speaking about. Notice also that "ye received the spirit of adoption." The Greek word for "adoption" there is *huiothesia*, which literally means "son-placing." When we're adopted, we're placed as sons. God adopts children who are servants (Galatians 4:1-7). A child is a servant but God adopts them as sons. "Sonship" is what we're growing into as we progressively bear more and more of the fruit of the Son, Jesus Christ. As the Son, Jesus Christ, comes to live in us, we manifest our sonship. So you're either submitted to the Spirit of God as a son, or you're under the spirit of bondage unto fear, as Romans 8:15 says. Fear is obviously bondage because it rules and reigns over people who have it; they cannot get control of themselves. Terror causes them to run rampant before the devil and be ruled-over by the devil. We're going to see very crazy things happen in this world because of fear in the days to come. We're going to see "Christians" who are not Christians because of fear.

All that God asks us to do is something that's already been paid for by the Lord. He's already delivered us out of the power of darkness and delivered us into the Kingdom of the Son of His love (Colossians 1:13). He wants us to walk by faith, and if we will walk by faith in Him, we will be able to cast down fear. We'll be able to "walk the walk" because faith gives us the power to do that. **(Heb.2:14) Since then the children are sharers in flesh and blood, he also himself in like manner partook of the same; that through death he might bring to nought him that had the power of death, that is, the devil** (The Lord came to deliver us from the power of death.)**; (15) and might deliver all them who through fear of death were all their lifetime subject to bondage.** It's obvious that because of the fear of death, the worldly do the things that they do. They're in bondage, but Christians are not supposed to be in that bondage. Jesus came to deliver us from the fear of death so that we wouldn't, all of our life, be subject to bondage and He accomplished that. He bore our sins upon Himself (2 Corinthians 5:21), and one of the sins, as we've seen from Revelation 21, is fear. He bore the sin of fear. You don't have to put up with fear because He delivered you from that darkness. He bore upon Himself that curse and so we don't have to live in fear. We have authority over fear because of what Jesus did at the Cross. We don't have to serve fear. We can say "No!" to fear. We can just rebuke fear, deny fear, refuse to listen to fear. We have <u>total</u> authority over fear.

The fear of death, many times, causes us to do things that we wouldn't normally do. I remember when my oldest son was being born at home, and we discovered that he was breach. I tell you, it was like the devil was waiting for me to see that little toe come out first to just jump on me with the spirit of fear. Of course, the devil tells you everything that's going to happen unless you go back to trusting in man, unless you go back to doing it the way of the world, but the Lord had led me to do this. He wanted me to have a lesson of trusting in Him. So I saw that little toe and I felt that spirit of fear come in that room. The first thing I did was say, "We're going to stop right here. We're going to pray and make war against this spirit." And we did; we commanded that demon to "Go, in the Name of Jesus Christ," and he did. And then we were no longer in bondage because of this fear of death.

The fear of death could be more than just fear of physical death. Many people fear death-to-self. They fear giving up their old life. In that case, the devil is able to keep us in bondage, keep us running to the world and the ways and methods of the world, but we know Jesus came to set us free from that. Jesus gave us authority over fear. Now if you're walking in willful sin, you'll have no boldness (1 John 3:21) and you won't be able to deny fear; it will overcome you. However, if you're not walking in willful sin, you're walking by faith in God and you have authority over fear. You can cast fear down and it will have to submit to you because of what Jesus said. **(Luk.10:19) Behold, I have given you authority to tread upon serpents and scorpions, and over all the power of the enemy: and <u>nothing</u> shall in any wise hurt you.** One thing we can do to conquer fear is we just refuse to listen. And so our son was born a footling breach, one foot up and one foot down, and of course, the doctors always do a Caesarean when that happens; they never birth a baby that way. Some people don't think it's even possible to do that, but after we ran the spirit of fear off, I told that baby to "Come out in the Name of Jesus!" and he was born a footling breach. You see, God can do anything, folks! Glory be to God!

His power is absolutely, totally, awesome, but we have to have our wits about us to be able to manifest it and if you have fear, you don't have boldness. If you have fear, you have faith in the devil and faith in the curse. As I just mentioned, one thing we should never do is listen to the voice of the devil. **(Psa.55:3) Because of <u>the voice of the enemy</u>, Because of the oppression of the wicked; For they cast iniquity upon me, And in anger they persecute me. (4) My heart is sore pained within me: And the terrors of death are fallen upon me.** "Because of the voice of the enemy" all these other things are true, including "the terrors of death." **(5) Fearfulness and trembling are come upon me, And horror hath overwhelmed me.** This is because of <u>lis-</u>

tening to the voice of the enemy instead of casting down these thoughts (2 Corinthians 10:5), these fiery darts, he shoots at us (Ephesians 6:16). We need to pray that God will always bring to our remembrance the things that He has said unto us (John 14:26), and then He will keep us in perfect peace. ***(Isa.26:3) Thou wilt keep [him] in perfect peace, [whose] mind [is] stayed [on thee;] because he trusteth in thee.*** We hold fast to the Word. We recognize that these thoughts, this "voice," is the devil because we know, "God hasn't given me a spirit of fear, this is the devil. Now I can stop, I can take authority, I can have victory over this. I do not have to listen to this as though it were me, because <u>it's not me</u>."

Listen To the Good Report

We've been delivered from fear and the Bible tells us that we should fill ourselves with ***(Php.4:8) ... whatsoever things are <u>true</u>*** (We know that when the spirit of fear comes, he's telling us a lie, something that's contrary to the Scriptures, and we're not supposed to listen to it.)***, whatsoever things are <u>honorable</u>, whatsoever things are <u>just</u>, whatsoever things are <u>pure</u>, whatsoever things are <u>lovely</u>, whatsoever things are of <u>good report</u>...*** Remember that it was the ten spies' bad report that caused the people's hearts to melt (Numbers 13:31-33,14:1-2; Joshua 14:8). They feared because of the bad report. Well-meaning people can bring us a "bad report," too, but if it's contrary to God's Word, we need to cast it out and cast it down. Be careful whenever you're making some man or medicine or doctors your god and they bring you the bad report. How can you be sick when by the stripes of Jesus you <u>were</u> healed (1 Peter 2:24)? You <u>can't</u> be sick because you <u>were</u> healed. Cast it down! Cast that bad report down because if fear causes you to accept that, then you have it. Jesus said, **(Mat.9:29) ... *According to your faith be it done unto you.***

What happens when somebody brings you that bad report? If you accept it, fear jumps on you because the devil knows that you're going to have a testimony if you continue in your faith. He attacks you to keep you from being delivered from this curse, delivered out of this darkness. He attacks you to keep you from walking by faith in the Lord, and what does the Lord tell us to do? ***(Php.4:8) Finally, brethren, whatsoever things are true, whatsoever things are honorable, whatsoever things are just, whatsoever things are pure, whatsoever things are lovely, whatsoever things are of good report; if there be any virtue, and if there be any praise, <u>think on</u> these things.*** The Greek there is *logízomai* and means "'take into account' these things." ***(Php.4:9) The things which ye both learned and received and heard and saw in me, these things do: and the <u>God of peace</u> shall be with you.***

Yes, you will have the God of peace with you, but we have a warfare to fight, folks. We are to be ***(2Cor.10:5) casting down imaginations, and every high thing that is exalted against the knowledge of God, and bringing every thought into captivity to the obedience of Christ.*** If you learn to bring "every thought into captivity to Christ," fear will never have a foothold and you will conquer it. God is omnipotent to work in us to will and to do of His good pleasure (Philippians 2:13). We don't have to give-in to the thoughts from the devil. We can cast them down. He said, "Because of the voice of the enemy ... the terrors of death are fallen upon me." Remember, that is the voice of the enemy, that is the devil, and you don't have to put up with it when he comes to you bringing the bad report and trying to put those thoughts of fear into your mind.

Some of you have not only listened to, but have read, things that are bringing fear into your life. Well, just as we are not to listen to the voice of the devil, we are not to read the voice of the devil, because these things can put fear in your heart. Some of you are studying things that are putting fear in you instead of building faith in you for the days to come. **(Isa.8:9) *Make an uproar, O ye peoples, and be broken in pieces; and give ear, all ye of far countries: gird yourselves, and be broken in pieces; gird yourselves, and be broken in pieces.*** A great tumult is coming over the world in these days, folks. **(10) *Take counsel together, and it shall be brought to nought; speak the word, and it shall not stand: for <u>God is with us</u>.*** "Emmanu-el" is with us. It is not our power, it's His power in us. It's Christ in us Who is the only hope of glory (Colossians 1:27). **(11) *For the Lord spake thus to me with a strong hand, and instructed me not to walk in the way of this people, saying, (12) Say ye not, A conspiracy, concerning all whereof this people shall say, A conspiracy; neither fear ye their fear, nor be in dread [thereof].*** I know Christians who study conspiracies all the time, and all it's doing is just filling their heart with fear. They don't have any faith towards God; they don't have any boldness towards God. They're afraid of the things that are coming upon the world because they're being disobedient.

Anxiety and Fear, Part 2

It doesn't matter, folks, who is behind the things that are coming upon the world. The Lord is ultimately behind it all because the Bible says that He works all things after the counsel of His Own Will (Ephesians 1:11). He was behind what came to Job. Standing back and looking at Job's situation, we see that we shouldn't fear because God Almighty is in control. If you're studying these conspiracies and you conclude that men are out to do you in, you're wrong. It's the devil who's out to do you in. You're wasting your time studying what men are trying to do because it is God Almighty Who's behind it, and His purpose is good for you. **(Rom.8:28) And we know that to them that love God all things work together for good, even to them that are called according to his purpose.** His purpose is to bring you into repentance and to faith in Him. So if you're studying men and are worried about what they might be doing and thinking that you have to do something about it, then you're getting in the flesh, all because you studied these conspiracies.

(Isa.8:12) Say ye not, A conspiracy, concerning all whereof this people shall say, A conspiracy; neither fear ye their fear, nor be in dread [thereof]. (13) The Lord of hosts, him shall ye sanctify; and let him be your fear, and let him be your dread. Why does the Lord say this? He says this because He is the One Who is ultimately in control, not the world, not the wicked, not the Illuminati, not anybody else. He is in control, and He promises us that **(Pro.16:7) When a man's ways please the Lord, He maketh even his enemies to be at peace with him.** So the Lord has absolute control over our enemies. He has control over every detail of our life and we need to put our trust in Him. We need to cast down these things that are bringing fear into our life because they're putting our sight on men. The Bible says, ***(Pro.29:25) The fear of man bringeth a snare; But whoso putteth his trust in the Lord shall be safe. (26) Many seek the ruler's favor; But a man's judgment [cometh] from the Lord.*** If you're afraid of man, then you are going to find yourself trapped in bondage again. And so, since "The fear of man bringeth a snare," don't study the conspiracies. Study what God has to say about what He will do to provide for you in the days to come. You shouldn't fear the things that are coming upon the world because that fear is for the devil's children, but the Lord is also going to use that fear to bring the wayward people of God to repentance and to trust in Him. Glory to God!

CHAPTER NINE

Steps You Can Take to be Immune from Plagues and Pestilences

With so many different plagues or pestilences spreading around, what can we do to protect ourselves and our families by God's power?

1) If you haven't done so already, ask Jesus to Give you His born-again Spirit so that you are entitled to the benefits of the Kingdom:

(Joh.3:3) Jesus answered and said unto him, Verily, verily, I say unto thee, Except one be born anew, he cannot see the kingdom of God.

(Eze.18:31) Cast away from you all your transgressions, wherein ye have transgressed; and make you a new heart and a new spirit: for why will ye die, O house of Israel? (Eze.36:26) A new heart also will I give you, and a new spirit will I put within you; and I will take away the stony heart out of your flesh, and I will give you a heart of flesh.

2) Ask God to fill you with His Holy Spirit for His supernatural power over the curse:

(Act.1:8) But ye shall receive power, when the Holy Spirit is come upon you: and ye shall be my witnesses both in Jerusalem, and in all Judaea and Samaria, and unto the uttermost part of the earth.

(Act.2:4) And they were all filled with the Holy Spirit, and began to speak with other tongues, as

the Spirit gave them utterance.

(Mar.16:17) And these signs shall accompany them that believe: in my name shall they cast out demons (Demons can also be spirits of infirmity or sickness, as in the Bible.); they shall speak with new tongues.

(Act.19:2) And he said unto them, Did ye receive the Holy Spirit when ye believed? And they said unto him, Nay, we did not so much as hear whether the Holy Spirit was given. ... (6) And when Paul had laid his hands upon them, the Holy Spirit came on them; and they spake with tongues, and prophesied.

(Act.4:31) And when they had prayed, the place was shaken wherein they were gathered together; and they were all filled with the Holy Spirit, and they spake the word of God with boldness.

(Act.13:52) And the disciples were filled with joy and with the Holy Spirit.

(Eph.5:18) And be not drunken with wine, wherein is riot, but be filled with the Spirit.

3) Repent and confess any sin so you can have faith to be healed:

(1Jn.1:7) But if we walk in the light, as he is in the light, we have fellowship one with another, and the blood of Jesus his Son cleanseth us from all sin. (8) If we say that we have no sin, we deceive ourselves, and the truth is not in us. (9) If we confess our sins, he is faithful and righteous to forgive us our sins, and to cleanse us from all unrighteousness.

(1Jn.3:20) Because if our heart condemn us, God is greater than our heart, and knoweth all things. (21) Beloved, if our heart condemn us not, we have boldness toward God; (22) and whatsoever we ask we receive of him, because we keep his commandments and do the things that are pleasing in his sight.

(Heb.10:26) For if we sin wilfully after that we have received the knowledge of the truth, there remaineth no more a sacrifice for sins, (27) but a certain fearful expectation of judgment, and a fierceness of fire which shall devour the adversaries. (28) A man that hath set at nought Moses' law dieth without compassion on [the word of] two or three witnesses.

(Jas.5:16) Confess therefore your sins one to another, and pray one for another, that ye may be healed.

4) Believe God's promises concerning sicknesses:
(1Pe.2:24) Who his own self bare our sins in his body upon the tree, that we, having died unto sins, might live unto righteousness; by whose stripes ye were healed.

(Psa.103:3) Who forgiveth all thine iniquities; Who healeth all thy diseases; (4) Who redeemeth thy life from destruction; Who crowneth thee with lovingkindness and tender mercies.

(Mar.11:23) Verily I say unto you, Whosoever shall say unto this mountain, Be thou taken up and cast into the sea; and shall not doubt in his heart, but shall believe that what he saith cometh

to pass; he shall have it. **(24) Therefore I say unto you, All things whatsoever ye pray and ask for, believe that ye receive them, and ye shall have them.**

(Jas.5:14) Is any among you sick? let him call for the elders of the church; and let them pray over him, anointing him with oil in the name of the Lord: (15) and the prayer of faith shall save him that is sick, and the Lord shall raise him up; and if he have committed sins, it shall be forgiven him. (16) Confess therefore your sins one to another, and pray one for another, that ye may be healed. The supplication of a righteous man availeth much in its working.

(Mat.18:19) Again I say unto you, that if two of you shall agree on earth as touching anything that they shall ask, it shall be done for them of my Father who is in heaven.

(Mar.16:17) And these signs shall accompany them that believe: in my name shall they cast out demons; they shall speak with new tongues; (18) they shall take up serpents, and if they drink any deadly thing, it shall in no wise hurt them; they shall lay hands on the sick, and they shall recover.

(Gal.3:13) Christ redeemed us from the curse of the law, having become a curse for us; for it is written, Cursed is every one that hangeth on a tree: (14) that upon the Gentiles might come the blessing of Abraham in Christ Jesus; that we might receive the promise of the Spirit through faith. Jesus bore the curse of sickness listed in Deuteronomy 28:15-68.

5) Believe in the authority that has been given to you by Jesus:

(Mat.28:18) And Jesus came to them and spake unto them, saying, All authority hath been given unto me in heaven and on earth. (19) Go ye therefore, and make disciples of all the nations, baptizing them into the name of the Father and of the Son and of the Holy Spirit: (20) teaching them to observe all things whatsoever I commanded you: and lo, I am with you always, even unto the end of the world. Notice here that everything that Jesus commanded the first disciples He also commands us.

(Mat.10:8) Heal the sick, raise the dead, cleanse the lepers, cast out demons: freely ye received, freely give. During the plagues, many will die. The Lord may instruct you to raise individuals from the dead. If so, boldly command it done and do not be double-minded.

(Jas.1:5) But if any of you lacketh wisdom, let him ask of God, who giveth to all liberally and upbraideth not; and it shall be given him. (6) But let him ask in faith, nothing doubting: for he that doubteth is like the surge of the sea driven by the wind and tossed. (7) For let not that man think that he shall receive anything of the Lord; (8) a doubleminded man, unstable in all his ways.

(Luk.9:1) And he called the twelve together, and gave them power and authority over all demons, and to cure diseases. ... (10:19) Behold, I have given you authority to tread upon serpents and scorpions, and over all the power of the enemy: and nothing shall in any wise hurt you. Use

that authority He gave you and cast out the spirits of sickness in the Name of Jesus.

(Joh.20:21) Jesus therefore said to them again, Peace [be] unto you: as the Father hath sent me, even so send I you. (Mat.18:18) Verily I say unto you, What things soever ye shall <u>***bind***</u> (Or, "forbid.") ***on earth shall be bound in heaven; and what things soever ye shall*** <u>***loose***</u> (Or, "permit.") ***on earth shall be*** <u>***loosed***</u> (Or, "permitted.") ***in heaven.***

(Col.1:13) Who delivered us out of the power of darkness, and translated us into the kingdom of the Son of his love.

(Job.22:28) Thou shalt also decree a thing, and it shall be established unto thee; And light shall shine upon thy ways.

6) Confess your salvation from sickness and your authority over it:

"Confess" is the Greek word *homologéō* and it means "to speak the same as." We must speak what God says about us and about our salvation from the curse of sickness and plague. And if we look at the examples given in Scripture for the noun *sótéria* meaning "salvation," and its verb *sōzō* meaning "saved," we see that this same word is used for physical healing, saving from difficult situations, and deliverance from demons of infirmity. Jesus saved us spirit, soul, and body, as He and His disciples demonstrated.

(Rom.10:10) For with the heart man believeth unto righteousness; and with the mouth confession is made unto salvation.

(Heb.3:1) Wherefore, holy brethren, partakers of a heavenly calling, consider the Apostle and

High Priest of our confession, [even] Jesus. Jesus offers our confession before the Father and the angels in order that we may receive the benefits of the Kingdom. *(Heb.4:14) Having then a great high priest, who hath passed through the heavens, Jesus the Son of God, let us hold fast our confession.*

(Mat.10:32) Every one therefore who shall confess me before men, him will I also confess before my Father who is in heaven. (Luk.12:8) And I say unto you, Every one who shall confess me before men, him shall the Son of man also confess before the angels of God. (1Ti.6:12) Fight the good fight of the faith, lay hold on the life eternal, whereunto thou wast called, and didst confess the good confession in the sight of many witnesses.

(Heb.10:23) Let us hold fast the confession of our hope that it waver not; for he is faithful that promised.

(Heb.13:15) Through him then let us offer up a sacrifice of praise to God continually, that is, the fruit of lips which make confession to his <u>name</u>. The Greek word for "name" means "nature, character, and authority."

(Act.3:6) But Peter said, Silver and gold have I none; but what I have, that give I thee. In the name of Jesus Christ of Nazareth, walk. The disciples commanded healing because it was already given by the sacrificial stripes of Jesus.

7) Health is given by God and may be declared for immunity <u>before</u> sickness comes:
(Exo.15:26) And he said, If thou wilt diligently

hearken to the voice of the Lord thy God, and wilt do that which is right in his eyes, and wilt give ear to his commandments, and keep all his statutes, I will put none of the diseases upon thee, which I have put upon the Egyptians: for I am the Lord that healeth thee.

(Exo.12:13) And the blood shall be to you for a token upon the houses where ye are: and when I see the blood, I will pass over you, and there shall no plague be upon you to destroy you, when I smite the land of Egypt.

(Psa.91:1) He that dwelleth in the <u>secret place of the Most High</u> (This is abiding in Christ through faith in His sacrifice for your sins and sickness.) *Shall abide under the shadow of the Almighty. (2) I will say of the Lord, He is my refuge and my fortress; My God, in whom I trust. (3) For he will deliver thee from the snare of the fowler, And from the deadly pestilence. (4) He will cover thee with his pinions, And under his wings shalt thou take refuge: His truth is a shield and a buckler. (5) Thou shalt not be afraid for the terror by night, Nor for the arrow that flieth by day; (6) For the pestilence that walketh in darkness, Nor for the destruction that wasteth at noonday. (7) A thousand shall fall at thy side, And ten thousand at thy right hand; [But] it shall not come nigh thee. (8) Only with thine eyes shalt thou behold, And see the reward of the wicked. (9) For thou, O Lord, art my refuge! Thou hast made the Most High thy habitation; (10) There shall no evil befall thee, Neither shall any plague come nigh thy tent. (11) For he will*

give his angels charge over thee, To keep thee in all thy ways. (12) They shall bear thee up in their hands, Lest thou dash thy foot against a stone. (13) Thou shalt tread upon the lion and adder: The young lion and the serpent shalt thou trample under foot. (14) Because he hath set his love upon me, therefore will I deliver him: I will set him on high, because he hath known my name. (15) He shall call upon me, and I will answer him; I will be with him in trouble: I will deliver him, and honor him. (16) With long life will I satisfy him, And show him my salvation.

8) According to these words from the Lord, declare immunity or healing boldly from your heart, and command the demons who administer the curse. You may command anything for which there is precedent in the Word, such as:

"I was healed by the stripes of Jesus!"
"No plague will come near my household!"
"Jesus bore my curse of sin and death!"
"I forbid plagues to come to this household, in Jesus' Name."
"Be healed in Jesus' Name!"
"I bind any plague from coming to me and my family, in Jesus' Name!"
"I claim the Blood of Jesus saves my household!"
"Go, Coronavirus, (or Ebola, Flu, etc.) in Jesus' Name!"

UBM BOOKS

www.ubmbooks.com

- ***Sovereign God For Us and Through Us*** by David Eells
- ***The Real Good News*** by David Eells
- ***Hidden Manna For the End Times*** by David Eells
- ***The Man-child and Bride Prophecy*** by David Eells
- ***Perfection Through Christ*** by David Eells
- ***How Shall We Die?*** by David Eells
- ***Destructive Demon Doctrines*** by David Eells
- ***The Tongue Conquers the Curse*** by David Eells
- ***Are You Following a Wolf?*** by David Eells
- ***Speak Grace, Not Condemnation*** by David Eells
- ***What Has Been Shall Be: The Man-child Returns*** by David Eells
- ***The Curse of Unforgiveness*** by David Eells
- ***Weakness, the Way to God's Power*** by David Eells
- ***Salvation: Instant and Progressive*** by David Eells
- ***Numeric English New Testament*** by Ivan Panin and UBM
- ***Beloved Spiritual Israel*** by David Eells
- ***Fear Not the Wilderness*** by David Eells
- ***Jesus Will Shepherd His Flock*** by David Eells
- ***Predestined, Called and Elect*** by David Eells
- ***Sanctification Before Blessing*** by David Eells
- ***Delivered From Dark Powers*** by David Eells
- ***Fear Not The Wilderness*** by David Eells
- ***God's Vaccine*** by David Eells
- ***Escape The Falling Away*** by David Eells
- ***The Word, Women and Authority*** by David Eells
- ***Saving Our Families By Grace*** by David Eells

Audio/Video Teachings Available For Free at www.ubm1.org